**New Directions for
Institutional Research**

Robert K. Toutkoushian
Editor-in-Chief

J. Fredericks Volkwein
Paul D. Umbach
Associate Editors

Institutional Research and Homeland Security

Nicolas A. Valcik

Editor

Number 146 • Summer 2010
Jossey-Bass
San Francisco

INSTITUTIONAL RESEARCH AND HOMELAND SECURITY
Nicolas A. Valcik (ed.)
New Directions for Institutional Research, no. 146
Robert K. Toutkoushian, Editor-in-Chief

NEW DIRECTIONS FOR INSTITUTIONAL RESEARCH (ISSN 0271-0579, electronic ISSN 1536-075X) is part of The Jossey-Bass Higher and Adult Education Series and is published quarterly by Wiley Subscription Services, Inc., A Wiley Company, at Jossey-Bass, 989 Market Street, San Francisco, California 94103-1741 (publication number USPS 098-830). Periodicals Postage Paid at San Francisco, California, and at additional mailing offices. POSTMASTER: Send address changes to New Directions for Institutional Research, Jossey-Bass, 989 Market Street, San Francisco, California 94103-1741.

SUBSCRIPTIONS cost $100 for individuals and $280 for institutions, agencies, and libraries in the United States. See order form at end of book.

EDITORIAL CORRESPONDENCE should be sent to Robert K. Toutkoushian, Educational Leadership and Policy Studies, Education 4220, 201 N. Rose Ave., Indiana University, Bloomington, IN 47405.

New Directions for Institutional Research is indexed in Academic Search (EBSCO), Academic Search Elite (EBSCO), Academic Search Premier (EBSCO), CIJE: Current Index to Journals in Education (ERIC), Contents Pages in Education (T&F), Current Abstracts (EBSCO), EBSCO Professional Development Collection (EBSCO), Educational Research Abstracts Online (T&F), ERIC Database (Education Resources Information Center), Higher Education Abstracts (Claremont Graduate University), Multicultural Education Abstracts (T&F), Sociology of Education Abstracts (T&F).

Microfilm copies of issues and chapters are available in 16mm and 35mm, as well as microfiche in 105mm, through University Microfilms, Inc., 300 North Zeeb Road, Ann Arbor, Michigan 48106-1346.

www.josseybass.com

For information about the Association for Institutional Research, write to the following address:

AIR Executive Office
1435 E. Piedmont Drive
Suite 211
Tallahassee, FL 32308-7955

(850) 385-4155

air@mailer.fsu.edu
http://airweb.org

CONTENTS

EDITOR'S NOTES

Since the attacks on September 11, 2001, new federal legislation and homeland security mandates have imposed stricter controls over research, increased data collection requirements, and required improved data integrity in information systems and new emergency management protocols from higher education institutions. At many colleges and universities, institutional researchers have inadvertently become the tip of the lance in contending with the effects of new compliance or regulatory statutes.

When an institutional research office becomes involved with homeland security issues, it is usually due to three key circumstances. First, an institutional research office is capable of observing all types of data from a holistic perspective. Second, an institutional research office often hires personnel with specific skills, such as computer programming, which enhance the office's capability for implementing homeland security measures. Third, an institutional research office regularly interfaces with the various departments, such as the registrar's office, for state or federal reporting and can expand these relationships to include homeland security efforts.

The chapter authors in this volume of *New Directions for Institutional Research* have either worked directly with homeland security issues or can advise institutional researchers and university administrators on contending with new and evolving legislative mandates (such as HAZMAT regulations) and existing statutes (such as Right to Privacy).

Since 2001, several incidents have caused federal and state governments to focus on universities as potential targets for terrorism, natural disasters, and random violence. This volume discusses how institutional research offices can provide data and research support to help their institutions comply with homeland security initiatives and their administrators mitigate the financial and cultural impact of these initiatives. Some of the chapters provide specific insights into newly enacted federal guidelines and how those guidelines may affect colleges and universities. Topics include the implementation and impact of SEVIS, new chemical inventory and security requirements, as well as other novel technologies to cope with new federal mandates. Additionally this volume will discuss new technologies that institutions can employ to assist with homeland security issues.

Threats from terrorist or criminal acts are not new to higher education. Events such as the Weatherman bombing of the Harvard

Center for International Affairs in 1970 and the Unabomber bombing of higher education facilities in the mid-1990s demonstrate the vulnerability of colleges and universities (Valcik, 2006). Universities have traditionally been open and accessible to students, staff, faculty, and the public. New federal guidelines that require greater security over research facilities, new policies to prevent data breaches, and increased reporting and data collection now challenge this open culture.

I would like to thank all of the authors and personnel who worked diligently on this volume. Without researchers and support staff this volume, and journal series for that matter, would not be possible.

Nicolas A. Valcik
Editor

Reference

Valcik, N. *Regulating the Use of Biological Hazardous Materials in Universities: Complying with the New Federal Guidelines.* Lewison, N.Y.: Edwin Mellen Press, 2006.

NICOLAS A. VALCIK is the associate director for the Office of Strategic Planning and Analysis and a clinical assistant professor for the Program of Public Affairs at The University of Texas at Dallas.

1

This chapter provides a framework for the volume by discussing ways that legislative mandates affect higher education institutions with regard to homeland security and the resulting cultural changes necessary at postsecondary institutions.

Issues in Homeland Security

Denise P. Sokol

Historically, higher education institutions in the United States have been subject to a broad variety of state and federal legislative and policy mandates that are sometimes at odds with the way academic institutions view themselves and the enterprise of postsecondary education. The core missions of postsecondary institutions revolve around teaching, research, service to the community, and values such as access, freedom, and the creation of new knowledge. The Higher Education Act, the Family Education Rights and Privacy Act, the Solomon Act, the Clery Act, and the reporting requirements of the Institutional Postsecondary Education Data Systems are just a few examples of the wide variety of legislative and policy mandates that postsecondary institutions have been subject to for many years and bear on the way higher education institutions do business. In order to respond to the requirements of legislative and policy mandates, institutions have developed business practices over time that affect a broad range of activities and academic and administrative processes such as admissions, enrollment, human resources, the research enterprise, and campus and information security.

When new legislation is enacted or amendments are made to existing legislation, institutions are required to review their business practices, policies, and procedures and make changes as necessary to maintain compliance. For example, on August 14, 2008, the Higher Education Opportunity Act was signed into law. This law reauthorizes and extends the Higher Education Act of 1965, as amended, which provides the authorizing legislation for most of the programs administered by the Office of

New Directions for Institutional Research, no. 146, Summer 2010 © Wiley Periodicals, Inc.
Published online in Wiley InterScience (www.interscience.wiley.com) • DOI: 10.1002/ir.339

Postsecondary Education, as well as for federal student aid programs. The 2008 reauthorization marks the eighth time the act has been amended. Each reauthorization requires institutions to examine the legislation and make changes to their procedures, policies, and business practices and adjust their data systems accordingly. This is but one example of the numerous laws that affect how higher education institutions do business. Institutional data systems, organizational structures, financial resources, and staffing are all affected when legislation is enacted or amended and are also factors in how slowly or quickly an institution is able to respond to changes. Especially in times of tight budgets, administrators face difficult decisions on funding the broad variety of activities of their institutions and are often faced with finding areas to cut. Unfortunately legislation usually does not include funding for implementation, but institutions have no choice but to comply with the legislative mandates, which sometimes means that already tight resources are stretched even further.

While postsecondary institutions are no strangers to the need to respond to legislative mandates, the tragic events that occurred on September 11, 2001, along with other instances of emergencies including Hurricane Katrina and the rise in shootings on college campuses, have resulted in the call for additional accountability and responsibility on the part of higher education institutions and have caused institutions themselves to examine procedures and policies in areas such as emergency management and communication. The establishment of the U.S. Department of Homeland Security and the passage of legislation such as the USA PATRIOT Act have created additional burdens for higher education institutions. New mandates take the form of increased reporting requirements, as well as the need to implement new and more restrictive campus and information security measures and practices. Balancing the additional requirements against core academic values such as openness, inclusiveness, freedom, and privacy present difficult challenges for higher education institutions.

Mark F. Smith provides a good summary of the provisions of the USA PATRIOT Act, which includes provisions affecting students and institutions of higher learning. The Patriot Act allows law enforcement agencies to track students, monitor electronic communications, and restrict research. The law "permits colleges and universities to disclose educational records to federal law enforcement officials, without the student's consent and without making a record of the disclosure, by amending FERPA [Family Educational Rights and Privacy Act]" (Smith, 2002).

Institutional research (IR) offices are often the locus for retrieving, analyzing, and reporting the information required for response and compliance because of institutional research's unique view of the entire academic enterprise and access to data that spans the institution. This volume examines the mandates related to homeland security and emergency management issues as they apply to higher education and especially focuses on how institutional research offices can help their institutions comply with the requirements of legislation enacted in response to increased threats of terrorism, natural disaster, and violence. This volume also includes coverage of issues such as the need to maintain confidentiality of data while simultaneously being responsive to requests for individually identifiable data in times of national crisis and emergency; the increase in threats to data stored in institutional data systems; the need for background checks for employees; how Student and Exchange Visitor System (SEVIS) implementation affects campuses; the use of geographic information systems for homeland security and emergency management in higher education institutions; how higher education institutions are affected by compliance, safety, and security issues related to chemical hazardous materials control; an examination of enrollment patterns related to natural disasters and campus violence; and a conclusion chapter that summarizes the information presented in the various chapters and offers some closing thoughts on the issues.

The following legislative mandates and standards that have an impact on higher education and institutional research are discussed in this volume:

- Census Statute, 1929
- Confidential Information Protection and Statistical Efficiency Act of 2002
- Coordinated Interagency Partnership Regulating International Students System
- Electronic Communication and Privacy Act
- Family Educational Rights and Privacy Act, 1974
- Federal Reports Act, 1942
- Homeland Security Act of 2002
- Illegal Immigration Reform and Immigrant Responsibility Act of 1996
- ISO 27002 Security Standards
- National Institute of Standards and Technology, 2009—National Vulnerability Database
- Privacy Act, 1974
- Public Health Security and Bioterrorism Preparedness and Response Act of 2002
- Second War Powers Act, 1942
- USA PATRIOT Act, 2001

Chapter Two traces the history of and tension between data collection by government agencies and the use of statistical data for administrative purposes, including the identification of individuals. Cathe Lester discusses the conflict between the need to ensure confidentiality in data collection and the pressure to disclose such data that occurs at the national level, especially in times of war or other national crises such as the terrorist attacks on September 11, 2001. Issues discussed include the principle of functional separation, statistical confidentiality and the U.S. Census Bureau, federal legislation with an impact on statistical confidentiality, and new federal legislation enacted to protect statistical confidentiality. Lester points out that institutional research (IR) offices must walk the tightrope of maintaining data confidentiality while providing reports that inform the campus on important issues every day, which gives these IR offices the experience to assist the campus in dealing with pressure from outside agencies to disclose confidential information in times of crisis. The author also provides some advice on how institutional researchers might approach the tricky ethical dilemma of being responsive and helpful to law enforcement agencies while still adhering to professional standards of conduct regarding data confidentiality.

In Chapter Three, William Custer provides a sobering and comprehensive look at information security issues in higher education and institutional research. The focus of Chapter Three is on the physical data stores of institutions, new threats to those data assets and methods to protect data from loss and misuse, the importance of clear information security governance, and the need for security planning. There is a discussion of the fact that organizational structures that exist in higher education are diverse, particularly related to institutional research's placement on the organization chart. This is important because of the access that institutional research office personnel have to sensitive individual data stored by institutions. Custer offers advice on how institutional research must work with the information technology department and the information security officer to ensure that data are protected.

Custer also provides startling statistics on the number of security breaches in higher education institutions and the implications of the exposure of institutional records. He offers detailed coverage of issues such as old and new hacking methods and regulations that exist regarding security breaches and the imperative to disclose the breaches to individuals; the additional problems created by the increased computing power of laptops and other portable devices, which make data stores portable and more vulnerable to theft; software application vulnerabilities and the pertinent federal mandates related to vulnerability management; and server infrastructure issues. The chapter concludes with a discussion of the need for information security governance and a security plan, which requires that institutional management understands the risk and allocates the resources necessary to protect institutional assets.

Chapter Four presents an examination of policies and procedures for background checks for students, faculty, and staff of higher education institutions related to homeland security issues and concerns. The authors (Stephanie Hughes, Eileen Weisenbach Keller, and Giles Hertz) provide an analysis of the increase in the use of background checks over recent years as higher education institutions seek to increase the safety of their students and employees. Included is a discussion of the lack of use of background checks for foreign faculty and students and the resulting gaps in safety enhancement, along with suggestions on how institutional research and planning offices can be of assistance in policy development in this area. The chapter covers statistics concerning the use of background checks by employers overall and in higher education specifically.

In the case of higher education, there is also an examination of the tension between the need to provide safety to students and employees and still protect the privacy of individuals. According to an article in *Academe Online*, blanket background checks provide little benefit to administrations, and often create a counterproductive atmosphere of distrust (Springer, 2003). The authors also review the legal issues related to background checks; how homeland security initiatives affect universities; the student visa process and background check processes; implications of the existing procedures and gaps related to background checks; and some final thoughts on whether the legislation enacted since 9/11 has improved campus and workplace safety.

Chapter Five covers the impact of homeland security mandates on institutions and international students and scholars. Author Janet Danley traces the history of interest by the Immigration and Naturalization Service in developing a management system for international students and scholars that eventually resulted in the birth of SEVIS in spite of protests from numerous higher education associations such as the American Council on Education and the American Association of Collegiate Registrars and Admissions Officers. Included in this chapter are discussions of the burden caused by the SEVIS unfunded mandate and review of SEVIS implementation by Washington State University, the University of Idaho, Lewis-Clark State College, and Walla Walla Community College. These reviews include discussion of how each institution chose to implement SEVIS and the impacts on the institutions. Also discussed are the institutional cultural changes created by SEVIS and the tension between providing a welcoming atmosphere for foreign students and scholars and the off-putting nature of SEVIS requirements and restrictions.

Chapter Six reviews the use of geographic information systems (GIS) to assist higher education systems with emergency procedures and plans. Author Stuart Murchison provides definitions of GIS and its use since 9/11 by government agencies and private businesses to "assess their infrastructure, attempt to identify and protect assets, integrate emergency operation centers with GIS, and use GIS in emergency response systems." The chapter explains the types of threats to higher education institutions, including natural disasters such as fires, floods, hurricanes, and tornadoes; threats to information technology assets and data; threats to chemical/radioactive and biological material; and threats of violence from humans. The chapter also examines why higher educational institutions lag in their use of GIS for emergency management purposes and offers suggestions to GIS

NEW DIRECTIONS FOR INSTITUTIONAL RESEARCH • DOI: 10.1002/ir

professionals in how they can make using GIS a viable option for post-secondary institutions.

In Chapter Seven Nicolas Valcik addresses hazardous materials (HAZMAT) use and storage at institutions of higher education and the impact of compliance, safety, and security issues of chemical HAZMAT control, especially in light of the Chemical Facility Anti-Terrorism Standards of the Homeland Security Appropriations Act of 2007. The chapter provides definitions of HAZMAT and focuses on chemical HAZMAT because of the increased scrutiny by the federal government of chemical substances that can be used to commit crimes or acts of terrorism if stolen. Included in this chapter is a discussion of how institutional research professionals can assist their institutions in developing methods to track and report on HAZMAT because of their unique access to pertinent data that exist in various databases across the institution and provides advice on what data should be gathered from the various sources. Included is an examination of government regulations over hazardous materials, especially the Homeland Security Chemical Facility Anti-Terrorism Standards of 2007, the PATRIOT Act of 2001, and the Bioterrorism Preparedness and Response Act of 2002. The chapter also covers the tension between the need to secure hazardous materials and facilities while maintaining the openness so valued by higher education and provides a review of HAZMAT policies and practices on various university campuses. Also included in the chapter is a review of a HAZMAT case study at one public research university and some closing thoughts on the ways that institutional research can assist other university offices in designing and implementing better HAZMAT plans and controls.

Chapter Eight provides a review of the impacts on enrollment after incidents at higher education institutions including natural disasters such as Hurricane Katrina and shootings on college campuses, which have been increasing. Author Hans L'Orange evaluates the impact of such disasters on the students themselves in both the short and long terms and on institutions related to enrollment patterns. The review includes a discussion of how institutional and state responses assisted students and how the incidents themselves prodded other institutions to implement improvements to emergency and communication procedures.

Chapter Nine by Dawn Kenney summarizes the preceding chapters and provides a discussion of the impacts of funded and unfunded mandates on higher education institutions' operations. It also raises questions about whether the mandates achieve the desired results.

A common theme among the chapters and topics in this volume is the tension between higher education's tradition of providing access and valuing openness and the legislative mandates to tighten policies, practices, and procedures in order to make certain that campuses are safe and secure places for students, faculty, staff, visitors, and the community as a whole. This volume provides a good introduction to the variety of legislation and policies that have been mandated since 9/11, how higher education has been affected, and how institutional research offices can be instrumental in assisting their institutions in implementing the legislative mandates. I suspect most reasonable people would agree that making campuses safe and secure and protecting valuable assets from harm is a worthy goal. Nevertheless, the tension between determining what is necessary to achieve the goal and what it will cost in terms of loss of privacy and other restrictions on personal freedom will continue to be a subject of debate for many years to come.

References

Smith, M. F. "Government Relations: Fighting Terrorism in a Free Society." *Academe Online,* Jan.-Feb. 2002. Retrieved June 20, 2009, from http://www.aaup.org/AAUP/pubres/academe/2002/JF/Col/gr.htm.

Springer, A. D. "Legal Watch-Background Checks: When the Past Isn't Past." *Academe Online,* Mar.-Apr. 2003. Retrieved June 23, 2009, from http://www.aaup.org/AAUP/pubres/academe/2003/MA/Col/LW.htm.

DENISE P. SOKOL *is a higher education consultant and retired assistant vice chancellor for institutional research, planning, and analysis at the University of Colorado Denver.*

NEW DIRECTIONS FOR INSTITUTIONAL RESEARCH • DOI: 10.1002/ir

2

This chapter briefly reviews the history of statistical confidentiality in the U.S. Census Bureau, the tension between statistical confidentiality and the need for information in the current national security environment, and the importance of institutional researchers' awareness and active participation in the debate surrounding confidentiality.

The Tension Between Data Confidentiality and National Security in Higher Education

Cathe Lester

> In both Democratic and Republican administrations, executive branch officials and the courts have, when faced with competing public needs, been disinterested in supporting, if not openly hostile to, the protection of statistical confidentiality.
>
> —Margo Anderson and William Seltzer (2009, p. 41)

Institutional researchers are responsible for the collection, organization, analysis, and maintenance of large amounts of personally identifiable data on students, faculty, and staff. Not only are institutional research (IR) offices required to report these data to state and federal agencies, they are also responsible for providing information to campus leaders to assess institutional effectiveness, assist in grant evaluation, or comply with outside requests for information. The importance of safeguarding and maintaining the confidentiality of data is quite clear in the professional codes of ethics that guide the IR profession, and researchers are aware of the principle of confidentiality inherent in the use of these data (Anderson and Seltzer, 2009).

Implicit in the term *confidentiality* is the belief that data collected for statistical purposes will be protected against disclosure to unauthorized users. The efforts to protect the confidentiality of statistical data have a long history in the federal statistical system, especially in the U.S. Census

NEW DIRECTIONS FOR INSTITUTIONAL RESEARCH, no. 146, Summer 2010 © Wiley Periodicals, Inc.
Published online in Wiley InterScience (www.interscience.wiley.com) • DOI: 10.1002/ir.340

Bureau. Historically, efforts to strengthen federal policies and laws of statistical confidentiality have been in reaction to the use of confidential statistical data for administrative or regulatory purposes during times of national crisis (Anderson and Seltzer, 2009). The attempt to protect the confidentiality of statistical data in times of national crisis continues today.

This chapter briefly reviews the history of statistical confidentiality within the Census Bureau, the uneven progression of policies and laws to protect statistical confidentiality, and the use of confidential data during times of national crisis. In addition, it introduces the newly implemented federal law, the E-Government Confidential Information Protection and Statistical Efficiency Act of 2002, to protect confidentiality of statistical data and notes the continuing tension between federal statistical and administrative agencies on the use of statistical data.

Statistical Confidentiality

By definition, statistical confidentiality encompasses three requirements (Fellegi, 1972). First, statistical data should be used only for statistical purposes (for example, reporting aggregated data or averages), protecting individuals or others who provide those data from harm. Second, only the staff of the statistical agency that collected the data should view and work with the data. Staff are subject to some penalty for divulging individually identifiable data—those associated with specific individuals or businesses who submitted data. Finally, statistical data should not be released in an identifiable format (Fellegi, 1972). Statisticians and researchers have always been concerned about the importance of ensuring confidentiality of statistical data collected and reported (Anderson and Seltzer, 2009; Fienberg, 1994). Early statisticians both within and outside the federal statistical system understood that assurances of confidentiality had to be honored to maintain the public trust of individuals and businesses providing census data (Anderson and Seltzer, 2009; Fienberg, 1994; Kirkendall, 1993; Watts, 1993). Without public trust, the quantity and the quality of the data collected would be reduced (Anderson and Seltzer, 2009; Fienberg, 1994; Kirkendall, 1993; Watts, 1993). Statistical agencies may struggle to convince individuals and other entities (e.g., businesses) to participate in surveys, federal or otherwise, due to the tenuous relation between privacy concerns and the provision of confidential information (Duncan, de Wolf, Jabine, and Straf, 1993). In fact, in an attempt to understand the low response rate to the 2000 Census, researchers found that individuals' concerns about privacy and confidentiality significantly predicted the return of census forms (Singer, Van Hoewyk, and Neugebauer, 2003).

NEW DIRECTIONS FOR INSTITUTIONAL RESEARCH • DOI: 10.1002/ir

The Principle of Functional Separation

Statisticians within and outside federal statistical agencies have argued that there should be a "functional separation" for how statistical data are used (Fienberg, 1994). The principle of functional separation proposes that statistical data (used for description, analysis, or estimation but without identifying individuals) should never be used for administrative purposes (Duncan, Jabine, and de Wolf, 1993; Fienberg, 1994). Administrative purposes would include "regulatory, law enforcement, adjudicatory, or other purpose that affects the rights, privileges, or benefits of a particular respondent" (Anderson and Seltzer, 2009; Implementation Guidance for Title V, 2007, p. 33364).

Statistical data are collected for statistical uses such as "the collection, compilation, processing, or analysis of information for statistical purposes" (Implementation Guidance for Title V, 2007, p. 33364). Statistical purposes would include, for example, aggregated descriptions of a group of individuals or businesses that could be used for policy development (Duncan, Jabine, and de Wolf, 1993). Statistical data should not be used by administrative agencies (such as the U.S. Justice Department or Internal Revenue Service) to make determinations about an individual (Duncan, Jabine, and de Wolf, 1993).

The principle of functional separation is adhered to by most statisticians, researchers, and federal statistical agencies such as the Census Bureau; however, functional separation has historically not been upheld by government officials and administrative agencies charged with enforcing the laws or protecting the nation (Anderson and Seltzer, 2009). For example, a breach in the principle of functional separation occurred in the late 1980s when the Justice Department's Antitrust Division requested individually identifiable data (that is, data associated with specific businesses) that companies had submitted to the Energy Information Administration (EIA; Duncan, de Wolf, Jabine, and Straf, 1993; Fienberg, 1994). The EIA refused to disclose the data, relying on its confidentiality policy. Although the Justice Department's legal counsel maintained that EIA should release the data, EIA refused. The Justice Department finally gave up its request; however, the inability of EIA to use its pledge of confidentiality raised concerns about the level of cooperation it would receive in future surveys (Duncan, de Wolf, Jabine, and Straf, 1993; Fienberg, 1994).

The misuse of statistical data for administrative purposes at the federal level has driven the establishment of federal policies and statutes protecting statistical confidentiality (Cecil, 1993). The need for statutes and policies protecting data confidentiality becomes highlighted during times of national crisis with the inability to maintain the principle of functional separation, and statistical confidentiality thus becomes more apparent (Anderson and Seltzer, 2009). The pressures to disclose confidential statistical data during times of national crisis can be seen clearly in the history of the Census Bureau.

Statistical Confidentiality and the U.S. Census Bureau

Over time, there has been a general tendency for federal statistical agencies to strengthen the statutory protections governing the confidentiality of data (Anderson and Seltzer, 2005, 2009). Since its establishment in 1902, the Census Bureau has recognized that the response rate and the quality of census data could be adversely affected by a lack of trust in the pledge of confidentiality protecting data submitted on census surveys (Anderson and Seltzer, 2005; Potok and Gates, 2002). However, in times of national crisis or war, "patriotism" and "professional zeal" may prompt administrative agencies to dismiss functional separation and statistical confidentiality, allowing administrative agencies to use statistical data for administrative purposes (Anderson and Seltzer, 2009; Seltzer and Anderson, 2001, p. 495).

One of the first instances of using statistical data for administrative purposes occurred during World War I (WWI; Anderson and Seltzer, 2007, 2009). Prior to WWI, business data submitted to the Census Bureau were protected by a 1909 statute assuring confidentiality (Anderson and Seltzer, 2007, 2009). Separately, individual-level census data were protected by a proclamation by President William H. Taft stating that "the census has nothing to do with taxation, with army or jury service . . . or with the enforcement of any national, State, or local law or ordinance, nor can any person be harmed in any way by furnishing the information required" (quoted in Anderson and Seltzer, 2009, p. 12).

At the outset of WWI, administrative agencies (whose jobs included collecting taxes and enforcing laws) and some members of Congress argued that assurances of confidentiality covered under the 1909 statute applied only to business data and that the presidential proclamation assuring the confidentiality of population data was not binding (Anderson and Seltzer, 2009). When President Woodrow Wilson's administration challenged the statistical confidentiality of population data collected by the Census Bureau, the administration won and mandated that the Census Bureau provide the names and ages of young men from the 1910 Census to "courts, draft boards, and the Justice Department" to pursue draft dodgers (quoted in Anderson and Seltzer, 2007, p. 7).

After WWI, the statistical confidentiality of business data collected by the Census Bureau continued to be challenged (Anderson and Seltzer, 2009). During that period, Census Bureau officials complied with multiple requests from administrative agencies charged with tax enforcement to provide confidential business data. Fearful of losing public trust in their pledges of confidentiality, the Census Bureau lobbied Congress to extend confidentiality assurances to all statistical data collected by the bureau.

NEW DIRECTIONS FOR INSTITUTIONAL RESEARCH • DOI: 10.1002/ir

Congress eventually passed the 1929 Census Statute, giving the director of the Census Bureau the discretion to refuse to provide business and population data to administrative agencies that would use them to the "detriment of the person or persons to whom such information relates" (quoted in Anderson and Seltzer, 2007, p. 10). Still, the pressure by administrative agencies to use statistical data collected by the Census Bureau and the efforts to strengthen statutory regulations protecting statistical confidentiality continued into World War II (WWII; Anderson and Seltzer, 2007, 2009).

At the start of WWII in 1939, statistical confidentiality was again challenged by the Justice Department, some members of Congress, and Roosevelt administration officials (Anderson and Seltzer, 2007, 2009); two new laws were enacted in 1942 (Anderson and Seltzer, 2009). The Federal Reports Act established standardized rules for data sharing among federal agencies. The Second War Powers Act amended the 1929 Census Statute and again allowed disclosure of confidential data collected by the Census Bureau "for use in connection with the conduct of war" (Anderson and Seltzer, 2009, p. 16). Confidential data were provided to defense and intelligence agencies charged with preparing the country for war (Anderson and Seltzer, 2007, 2009). Recently it has been suggested that confidential statistical data collected by the Census Bureau were ultimately used in the internment of Japanese Americans during WWII (Anderson and Seltzer, 2007, 2009; Seltzer and Anderson, 2001).

Federal policies and laws protecting statistical confidentiality of census data were developed in response to challenges by administrative agencies such as the Justice Department that requested and received census data for administrative purposes (pursuit of draft dodgers in WWI and preparing the nation for war in WWII; Anderson and Seltzer, 2009). Statutes and presidential proclamations assuring confidentiality of census data were amended in World Wars I and II, weakening statistical confidentiality and leaving the Census Bureau and other federal statistical agencies vulnerable (Anderson and Seltzer, 2009; Seltzer and Anderson, 2001).

Attempts to strengthen statistical confidentiality at the federal level have been ongoing over the past several decades (Anderson and Seltzer, 2009). One source of difficulty in maintaining statistical confidentiality across federal statistical agencies has been the decentralized nature of those statistical agencies (Duncan, de Wolf, Jabine, and Straf, 1993). Furthermore, the level of statutory protections of confidentiality is regulated not by comprehensive statutes across the federal statistical system, but by the statutory authority of the agency that collects and maintains the data (Cecil, 1993). In times of national crisis or war, the vulnerability of statistical agencies to disclose statistical data to administrative agencies increases (Anderson and Seltzer, 2009). Thus, it is not surprising that the uncomfortable tension among statistical confidentiality, need to know, and information sharing returned to the forefront after the attacks of

September 11, 2001 (Anderson and Seltzer, 2009). After 9/11, institutions of higher education, storehouses of student and faculty records, were asked to provide data to federal law enforcement agencies. While encouraged to do so whenever possible, institutions were cautioned to do so within existing laws (Rodgers, 2002). Institutional research offices were now confronted with making the same decisions between confidentiality and information sharing encountered at the federal level.

Federal Legislation With an Impact on Statistical Confidentiality in Higher Education

Institutions of higher education face the same tensions between statistical confidentiality and information sharing found across federal agencies. In 1974, the Privacy Act was passed to prevent government intrusion into individual records (Anderson and Seltzer, 2007, 2009; Duncan, Jabine, and de Wolf, 1993). Data were to be used only for the purpose for which they were collected (Anderson and Seltzer, 2007, 2009; Privacy Act Implementation, 1975). However, the Privacy Act provided little protection from improper disclosure of statistical data, and even after enactment, statistical confidentiality at the federal level continued to be governed by separate, individual policies and statutes specific to an agency (Cecil, 1993; Duncan, Jabine, and de Wolf, 1993).

The Family Educational Rights and Privacy Act (FERPA), enacted in 1974, was an attempt to prevent disclosure of confidential student educational records, except for directory information, that is, student information contained in an educational record that would not be considered harmful if disclosed (FERPA, Subpart A, Section 99.3). Directory information includes such items as the student's name, address, telephone listing, date and place of birth, major field of study, and dates of attendance, and so on (FERPA, Subpart A, Section 99.3). Nondirectory information would include any personally identifiable information including any "personal characteristics that would make a student's identity easily traceable" (FERPA, Subpart A, Section 99.3). Under FERPA, nondirectory information can be released only with a court order (Rodgers, 2002). The limited protection of confidentiality provided by the Privacy Act and FERPA weakened even further after the attacks of September 11, 2001.

After 9/11, national security issues became dominant at local, state, and federal levels (National Commission on Terrorist Attacks, 2004). Local, state, and federal government agencies needed to have the ability to collaborate and share information effectively in order to identify and investigate suspected terrorists and to prevent further terrorist attacks (National Commission on Terrorist Attacks, 2004; Markle Foundation Task Force, 2009). In fact, the 9/11 Commission identified the lack of information sharing among federal intelligence agencies as a primary factor leading to the failure to prevent the attacks (National Commission on

Terrorist Attacks, 2004). The commissioners' recommendations to prevent additional terrorist attacks included calls for increased information sharing among federal, state, and local law enforcement and intelligence agencies (National Commission on Terrorist Attacks, 2004; Markle Foundation Task Force, 2009).

Although the Privacy Act of 1974 had prevented most government intrusion into personal information held by federal government agencies up to this point and FERPA had similarly prevented disclosure of confidential student data, a waning of statistical confidentiality was observed after 9/11 (Anderson and Seltzer, 2009). Less than one week after the attacks, the USA PATRIOT Act was drafted (National Commission on Terrorist Attacks, 2004). At that time, Attorney General John Ashcroft voiced his commitment to "take every conceivable action, within the limits of the Constitution, to identify potential terrorists and deter additional attacks" (National Commission on Terrorist Attacks, 2004, p. 345). Although the 9/11 Commission cautioned the administration on the importance of "safeguarding the privacy of individuals about whom information is shared" (National Commission on Terrorist Attacks, 2004, p. 412), administrative agencies such as the Justice Department understandably argued that information sharing was the most critical part of fighting the "war on terrorism" (National Commission on Terrorist Attacks, 2004).

For institutions of higher education, the most relevant section of the Patriot Act was section 508 (Seltzer and Anderson, 2002). Previously section 408 of the 1994 National Education Statistics Act (NESA) had protected the confidentiality of individual-level data submitted to the National Center for Educational Statistics (NCES). Section 408 of NESA was amended by section 508 of the 2001 Patriot Act (Anderson and Seltzer, 2009; Seltzer and Anderson, 2002; Patriot Act, PL 107-56, Section 508). Institutions of higher education submit aggregated data to NCES's Integrated Postsecondary Education Data System (IPEDS) annually (Seltzer and Anderson, 2002). In addition, some postsecondary institutions have submitted population lists of students (used by NCES for sampling frames) containing individually identifying information to NCES for use in large federal surveys such as the National Post-Secondary Student Aid Study (Seltzer and Anderson, 2002). Section 508 of the Patriot Act affects these data.

Specifically, section 508 allows the Justice Department to use an *ex parte* order to request and use individual-level data submitted by institutions of higher education to NCES in the "investigation or prosecution" of terrorists (Seltzer and Anderson, 2002; see section 508(c)(1)(A) of PL 107-56, 2001). In addition, section 508 prevents prosecution of NCES staff who provide that information to the Justice Department (Seltzer and Anderson, 2002; see section 508(2)(B)(3), PL 107-56). Section 508 is vague on whether data collected only after enactment are vulnerable or if data collected prior to enactment also can be included in requests from the Justice Department; no one at the federal level has ever acknowledged how or if these confidential data may have been used (Seltzer and Anderson, 2002). Notably section 508 did not expire when other provisions of the Patriot Act expired, essentially codifying the weakening of statistical confidentiality (Seltzer and Anderson, 2002).

Part of the difficulty with maintaining statistical confidentiality in the federal statistical system has stemmed from the lack of uniform, comprehensive statutes governing statistical data confidentiality and use (Anderson and Seltzer, 2009). For example, in section 4-2 of NCES's Statistical Standards, statistical confidentiality is governed by five laws: (1) the Privacy Act of 1974, as amended, (2) the E-Government Act of 2002 (Title V, Subtitle A, Confidential Information), (3) the Education Sciences Reform Act of 2002, (4) the Federal Statistical Confidentiality Order of 1997, and (5) the Patriot Act (National Center for Education Statistics, 2002). The patchwork of policies and laws protecting statistical confidentiality in federal statistical agencies leaves those agencies vulnerable to pressures to disclose confidential data for uses other than what they were collected for, especially during times of national crisis or war (Cecil, 1993; Anderson and Seltzer, 2009).

Federal statistical agencies, as well as postsecondary IR offices, understand the importance of maintaining the confidentiality of their data and know that if confidentiality pledges are not honored, the resulting lack of trust could compromise the quality and completeness of data that are collected and the reports produced from those data (Duncan, de Wolf, Jabine, and Straf, 1993). With new federal legislation passed soon after the Patriot Act, Congress, as the agency that defines underlying law governing statistical confidentiality, attempted to strengthen statistical confidentiality (Anderson and Seltzer, 2009).

New Federal Legislation Protecting Statistical Confidentiality

Title V of the E-Government Confidential Information Protection and Statistical Efficiency Act of 2002 (CIPSEA; Title V, 2002) both addresses the importance of statistical data collection serving the "interests of the public and the needs of society" (Anderson and Seltzer, 2009, p. 40) and attempts to ensure public trust in the gathering of statistical data (Anderson and Seltzer, 2009). The "findings" (Anderson and Seltzer, 2009, p. 40) issued by the Office of Management and Budget (OMB) in 2007 state: "(2) Pledges of confidentiality by agencies provide assurances to the public that information about individuals or organizations or provided by individuals or organizations for exclusively statistical purposes will be held in confidence and will not be used against such individuals or organizations in any agency action" (PL 107-347, Subtitle A, Sec. 511(a)(2)).

In addition, subsection A of CIPSEA clearly defines statistical and nonstatistical purposes for data and provides guidance on when data should be considered confidential. Statistical purposes include the "description, estimation, or analysis of the characteristics of groups, without identifying the individuals or organizations that comprise such groups" (Implementation Guidance for Title V, 2007, p. 33364). Nonstatistical purposes include any "administrative, regulatory, law enforcement, adjudicatory, or other purpose that affects the rights, privileges, or benefits of a particular respondent" (Implementation Guidance for Title V, 2007, p. 33364).

CIPSEA also states that statistical data acquired and protected under CIPSEA may be used only for statistical purposes and any agency that directly acquires information from a respondent under a pledge of confidentiality for exclusively statistical purposes is bound by CIPSEA (Implementation Guidance for Title V, 2007). In addition, "information collected or maintained for statistical purposes must never be used for administrative or regulatory purposes or disclosed in identifiable form, except to another statistical agency with assurances that it will be used solely for statistical purposes" (Implementation Guidance for Title V, 2007, p. 33368).

In 2007, the Office of Management and Budget (OMB) released guidelines for implementation of CIPSEA in federal agencies (Anderson and Seltzer, 2009). The OMB expects the vast majority of data collection by statistical agencies to be subject to CIPSEA because these agencies generally collect such information exclusively for statistical purposes and provide pledges of confidentiality (Implementation Guidance for Title V, 2007). Although the OMB is a key player in the establishment of regulations governing statistical confidentiality and data access, Congress defines the mission of federal statistical agencies and establishes the underlying framework for issues of statistical confidentiality (Duncan, de Wolf, Jabine, and Straf, 1993).

In reviewing the historical trends in statistical confidentiality in the Census Bureau, it is unclear whether the provisions of CIPSEA will withstand future challenges of statistical confidentiality if the nation once again finds itself in crisis (Anderson and Seltzer, 2009). Notably, section 508 of the 2001 Patriot Act did not expire along with the other provisions of the act and still allows NCES to share confidential data with the U.S. Justice Department if those data are relevant to the investigation and prosecution of suspected terrorists (Anderson and Seltzer, 2009; Patriot Act, PL-107-56, section 508). Furthermore, FERPA has been amended under the Patriot Act, allowing the Justice Department to apply for a court order to "collect, retain, disseminate, and use certain education records in the possession of an educational agency or institution without regard to any other FERPA requirements, including in particular the record-keeping requirements" (Family Educational Rights and Privacy Act, 2008,

p. 74819). Although CIPSEA attempts to provide uniform, comprehensive protection of statistical confidentiality across federal statistical agencies, section 508 of the Patriot Act leaves CIPSEA vulnerable to challenges from administrative agencies, especially in times of national crisis (Anderson and Seltzer, 2009).

Conclusion

Similar to federal statistical agencies, the function of an IR office is to produce reports to support campus planning and improvement. The identification of individuals, carefully guarded with respect to security and statistical disclosure, is simply a tool used to produce these reports. The tension between the need for information to inform the campus and maintaining data confidentiality is felt in IR offices every day. Institutional researchers have to carefully balance the ethical obligation to safeguard the confidentiality of data and the need for information, both internal to the campus and to outside agencies.

Historically, the balance between the need for information and statistical confidentiality has shifted in federal agencies during times of crisis. Although it is understandable that information sharing is critical during a national crisis, the sharing must be balanced with policies and statutes that protect statistical confidentiality. Federal statistical agencies have attempted to develop uniform policies and legislative protections of statistical confidentiality; however, statistical data continue to become vulnerable to misuse in times of national crisis.

Institutional researchers are guided by codes of professional conduct and ethics such as those of the Association of Institutional Research and the American Statistical Association. These codes are a reminder of the obligation to safeguard confidential data in daily business and can assist when balancing choices between data sharing and statistical confidentiality. Institutional researchers should be aware of state and federal laws that govern the protection of data confidentiality. One support system that could assist in balancing choices between information sharing and data confidentiality would be a campus committee. This committee could develop uniform campus standards related to statistical confidentiality. In addition, the committee could keep the campus community aware of current and pending state and federal laws on statistical confidentiality, as well as the impact of those laws on campus operations. National discussions of institutional researchers would also provide support to those making choices between information sharing and statistical confidentiality. Although IR offices want to assist law enforcement agencies in times of national crisis, that assistance must be balanced against policies and laws that protect statistical confidentiality.

NEW DIRECTIONS FOR INSTITUTIONAL RESEARCH • DOI: 10.1002/ir

References

Anderson, M., and Seltzer, W. "Federal Statistical Confidentiality and Business Data: Twentieth Century Challenges and Continuing Issues." Paper presented at the meeting of the Federal Committee on Statistical Methodology, Arlington, Va., Nov., 2005.

Anderson, M., and Seltzer, W. "Challenges to the Confidentiality of U.S. Federal Statistics, 1910–1965." *Journal of Official Statistics*, 2007, *23*(1), 1–34.

Anderson, M., and Seltzer, W. "Federal Statistical Confidentiality and Business Data: Twentieth Century Challenges and Continuing Issues." *Journal of Privacy and Confidentiality*, 2009, *1*(1), 7–52. Retrieved Apr. 15, 2009, from http://jpc.cylab.cmu.edu/.

Cecil, J. S. "Confidentiality Legislation and the United States Federal Statistical System." *Journal of Official Statistics*, 1993, *9*(2), 519–535.

Duncan, G. T., de Wolf, V. A., Jabine, T. B., and Straf, M. L. "Report of the Panel on Confidentiality and Data Access." *Journal of Official Statistics*, 1993, *9*(2), 271–274.

Duncan, G. T., Jabine, T. B., and de Wolf, V. A. (eds.). *Private Lives and Public Policies: Confidentiality and Accessibility and Government Statistics.* Washington, D.C.: National Academy Press, 1993.

Family Educational Rights and Privacy Act; Final Rule, 73 (23) Fed. Reg. 74806, Dec. 2008. Retrieved Apr. 29, 2009, from http://www.worldprivacyforum.org/pdf/FERPA rule.pdf.

Fellegi, I. P. "On the Question of Statistical Confidentiality." *Journal of the American Statistical Association*, 1972, *67*(337), 7–18.

Fienberg, S. E. "Conflicts Between the Needs for Access to Statistical Information and Demands for Confidentiality." *Journal of Official Statistics*, 1994, *10*(2), 115–132.

Implementation Guidance for Title V of the E-Government Act, Confidential Information Protection and Statistical Efficiency Act of 2002 (CIPSEA); Notice. 72 (115) Fed. Reg. 33362, June 2007. Retrieved Apr. 28, 2009, from http://www.whitehouse .gov/omb/fedreg/2007/061507_cipsea_guidance.pdf.

Kirkendall, N. J. "Discussion: Statutes and Administration." *Journal of Official Statistics*, 1993, *9*(2), 591–593.

Markle Foundation Task Force on National Security in the Information Age. "Nation at Risk: Policy Makers Need Better Information to Protect the Country." 2009. Retrieved Apr. 20, 2009, from http://www.markletaskforce.org/.

National Center for Education Statistics. "NCES Standard 4-2, Subject: Maintaining Confidentiality." 2002. Retrieved Apr. 20, 2009, from http://nces.ed.gov/statprog/ 2002/std4_2.asp.

National Commission on Terrorist Attacks Upon the United States. "9-11 Commission Final Report." Washington, D.C.: U.S. Government Printing Office, 2004. Retrieved Apr. 21, 2009, from http://www.gpoaccess.gov/911/index.html.

Potok, N. A., and Gates, G. W. "Data Stewardship and Accountability at the U.S. Census Bureau." Panel on Benefits and Stewardship of Linked Survey and Administrative Data, Federal Committee on Statistical Methodology Statistical Policy Seminar, Bethesda, Md., Nov. 2002.

Privacy Act Implementation, Guidelines and Responsibilities. 40 (132) Fed. Reg. 28943, July 1975. Retrieved Apr. 28, 2009, from http://edocket.access.gpo.gov/2006/ pdf/E6-10869.pdf.

Rodgers, S. "FERPA Compliance Update." 2002. Retrieved Apr. 21, 2009, from http:// www.aacrao.org/transcript/index.cfm?fuseaction=show_viewanddoc_id=1043.

Seltzer, W., and Anderson, M. "The Dark Side of Numbers: The Role of Population Data Systems in Human Rights Abuses." *Social Research*, 2001, *68*(2), 481–513. Retrieved Apr. 20, 2009, from www.uwm.edu/margo/govstat/integrity.htm.

Seltzer, W., and Anderson, M. "NCES and the Patriot Act: An Early Appraisal of Facts and Issues." Paper prepared for presentation at the Joint Statistical Meeting, New York City, Aug. 2002. Retrieved Apr. 21, 2009, from www.uwm.edu/ margo/govstat/ integrity.htm.

Singer, E., Van Hoewyk, J., and Neugebauer, R. J. "Attitudes and Behavior: The Impact of Privacy and Confidentiality Concerns on Participation in the 2000 Census." *Public Opinion Quarterly*, 2003, 67, 368–384.

Title V. Confidential Information Protection and Statistical Efficiency, P.L. No. 107-347, 116 Stat. 2962. 2002. Retrieved Apr. 20, 2009, from http://aspe.hhs.gov/datacncl/Privacy/titleV.pdf.

Uniting and Strengthening America by Providing Appropriate Tools Required to Interrupt and Obstruct Terrorism (USA PATRIOT Act), P.L. No. 107-56, 115 Stat. 272. 2001. Retrieved Apr. 20, 2009, from http://frwebgate.access.gpo.gov/cgi-bin/getdoc.cgi?dbname=107_cong_public_lawsanddocid=f:publ056.107.pdf.

Watts, H. W. "Discussion: Statutes and Administrative Procedures." *Journal of Official Statistics*, 1993, 9(2), 595–598.

CATHE LESTER *is an associate director for the Center for Institutional Evaluation, Research and Planning and lecturer in the College of Health Science for The University of Texas at El Paso.*

NEW DIRECTIONS FOR INSTITUTIONAL RESEARCH • DOI: 10.1002/ir

3

Increasing security threats, new and old, to the data assets of higher education require mitigation through an institutional security program based on risk assessment and grounded in clear governance.

Information Security Issues in Higher Education and Institutional Research

William L. Custer

Information security threats to educational institutions and their data assets have worsened significantly over the past few years. The rich data stores of institutional research are especially vulnerable, and threats from security breaches represent no small risk. New genres of threat require new kinds of controls if the institution is to prevent data loss. Nevertheless, risk from traditional threats must not be ignored, and traditional security planning based on risk is still the foundational strategy. Governance of the security function must be clearly established. Under three areas—human factors, software applications, and server infrastructure— this chapter examines a sampling of basic information security threats new and old to educational data assets, along with corresponding controls that will reduce risk. Finally the basics of a security plan are described.

Diversity of Governance

Data assets held by even a small educational institution are varied and valuable, and management of these assets by institutional research (IR) professionals follows no uniform governance standard. The wide variety of locations that IR is placed on a university organizational chart exhibits diverse management almost to the point of chaos. The image of chaos, though tongue-in-cheek, helps focus the question: How within the chaos of the IR governance can one practice good information security?

The Security Functions

Critical to good asset management is a complete set of security functions within the diverse governance standards of IR. Although variety in governance standards is part of the freedom that defines our educational heritage, this variety may help create the very cracks through which data assets leak. Data assets may leak that is, unless one takes a deliberate and structured approach to manage security through a complete set of information security functions.

What constitutes a set of security functions that is complete? Who is implementing them, and with what group of professionals will they network? From what body of knowledge will they obtain help? And to whom do they report? The exact location of IR management on the organizational chart is less important to security than ensuring that all security functions are present, assigned a place in the organization, and managed. A complete set of security functions is embodied in standards such as the ISO 27002, and from such standards a security program should be built. Thus, IR staff who secure data assets will need to work closely with security professionals who understand these standards. Who is the IR community, what kind of data assets do they manage, and what are the threats to these assets?

The IR Community

The IR community is that group whose research focuses on the identity and practices of educational institutions. At the core of IR is a common set of reports and the data sets that support them, including state and federal reporting such as IPEDS, external reports such as the U.S. News and World Report annual survey, internal reports such as audit reports or enrollment tracking, as well as ad hoc requests in great variety. To this definition of the IR community, we might add those who read journals like *New Directions for Institutional Research* and attend conferences such as the Association for Institutional Research (AIR) and the Rocky Mountain Association for Institutional Research (RMAIR). Although this definition could be improved, it is adequate to show that the IR community requires access to a wide variety of confidential data and in large quantities.

The IR Data Landscape

The data accessed by IR is varied and valuable and consequently requires competent protection and management. As IR professionals we know more than the Internal Revenue Service does about our institutional community. In addition to a financial profile of most parents, embedded in our data stores are profiles of all students: their interests; their successes;

their failures; where they live, eat, and sleep; and the places they frequent. We report on robberies and rapes, on suspensions and sicknesses, on mental health and suicide. We know where the hazardous materials on campus are stored. In some cases, this data is anonymized, but most of us could produce a list of names, birthdates, and social security numbers for about 80 percent (those who file the Free Application for Federal Student Aid) of our constituency. With this kind of access to information comes the responsibility for good asset management.

Note that institutional research is not to be confused with other research going on in the academy such as the causes of cancer or sleep deprivation. The subject of the former is the institution itself, whereas the subject of the latter ranges widely from physics to psychology, from microbiology to medicine. Research done by the academic disciplines is also an asset that requires protection; though it rarely holds social security numbers, it may be equally the target of theft or even espionage.

The IR Governance Landscape

The organizational charts used to manage the IR data landscape are almost as varied as the number of institutions represented. IR units vary in size from a one- or two-person office (or even a part-time person), to a medium department of five or six, and on to a mini data center. Among the names used are *institutional research, business intelligence, data mining, data warehousing,* and *organizational effectiveness/planning.* These offices are also governed in diverse ways: by the provost, a dean, by human resources, or even information technology.

IR Governance, Security, and Information Silos

The already complex life of the IR professional, who must deal with varied and valuable data and diverse governance is complicated further when information security is added. The challenge is particularly acute for the IR organization that manages its own servers and applications or has its own data center.

Moreover, information security governance for educational institutions is not uniform, magnifying the information silo effect through an even larger matrix of relationships between IR and the security function: IR reporting to X, seeking help from security reporting to Y, about assets on servers managed by Z. The information security function commonly resides in information technology (IT) which is also where the Information Technology Governance Institute places it (Tipton and Henry, 2007), but it may reside elsewhere in the organization.

The boundaries among IR, IT, and the information security officer vary from institution to institution. IR may have a data center, install Web servers, apply server patches, or even develop software and manage its own change control, but it will not likely manage a network; or IR may do none of these. Regardless of the governance pattern, security professionals and the IR professionals who share the security function face new and increasing challenges. One writer summed up the challenge that information silos pose to security risk as follows: "Security risk is not solely the consequence of an inexperienced IT staff or a lack of a mature process. . . . The problem lies in the fact that risk is typically handled by a multitude of functional teams which prevents system-wide risk management and restricts operations down to more of a device centric view" (Mayer, 2008, p. 11).

Security Breaches Increase New Incident Numbers

The number of security incidents among educational institutions continues to rise, resulting in significant cost. Adam Dodge (2009) has made available a body of helpful research on information security breaches in educational institutions. He notes that as far back as the late 1990s, educational institutions have been one of the most compromised industry sectors and that this trend continues today. From 2007 to 2008, the number of educational security incidents rose 24.5 percent to a total of 173 incidents. This continued the rise from 2006 to 2007 (Dodge, 2009). The number of educational institutions involved in security incidents continues to increase as well. The 178 institutions affected by security incidents in 2008 represents an increase of 59 percent over 2007 and 173 percent over 2006 (Dodge, 2009). The total number of records exposed by educational security incidents is also up from previous years, reaching 4,880,052 in 2008. This is an average of 78,710 records per incident for which records lost is given (Dodge, 2009). This average may be slightly misleading since two incidents of stolen backup tape led the list for number of records stolen and together involve 3.6 million records, for 73.8 percent of the total. After factoring out the two largest incidents, the average number of records per incident was 21,334.

Personally identifiable information continues to lead as the most exposed type of information (41.9 percent), followed by social security numbers (32.9 percent; Dodge, 2009). Personally identifiable information plus social security numbers together are involved in 74.8 percent of the incidents. These two types of information are likely to require notification, resulting in considerable cost to the institution.

New Threats, New Motives

Penetration, theft, and unauthorized disclosure were the leading types of information breach among educational institutions in 2008, comprising a full 86.7 percent(see Table 3.1). These incident types have been the leaders for some years now.

Table 3.1. Change in Incidents Reported in 2006, 2007, and 2008

Type of Incident	Reported in 2006	Reported in 2007	Reported in 2008
Employee fraud	0	1	10
Impersonation	1	3	4
Loss	3	13	9
Penetration	33	30	35
Theft	26	39	40
Unauthorized disclosure	20	53	75
Grand total	**83**	**139**	**173**

Source: Dodge (2009).

What is not stated in Table 3.1 is the apparent shift in motive and personal profile of penetration incidents. Five or six years ago, it was a standing joke among security professionals that the profile for computer penetration was of a teenager (often in some cold climate such as Scandinavia) seeking adventure or a reputation or a place to store stolen music, videos, or pornography. Today's penetration threats come from highly trained professional hackers, thieves, and political opportunists who have powerful motives, endless time, and significant resources (Goggans, 2008). The motive has shifted from adventure or enhancement of reputation to profit.

The new thieves assemble personal information from multiple breaches into databases of personal profiles and sell them on an open market. It is widely understood that many attacks originate in Russia or China, where industrial espionage and theft of personally identifiable information are rarely prosecuted (Brenner, 2009), as long as it is not practiced against them (Carr, 2008). Also widely understood is that many attacks originate from areas of the former Soviet Union and eastern bloc countries that had strong technical schools whose students cannot now find legitimate employment using their computer skills (Goggans, 2008). The involvement of the Russian mafia in these activities is also well known (Naraine, 2006), and law enforcement has attempted to end it (Carr, 2008).

Breach Security Labs reported that 67 percent of all attacks in 2007 were motivated by profit and that 40 percent of attacks were waged to harvest personal data (Breach Security Labs, 2007).

One rather bold example of the criminal motive is an extortion demand in 2009 seeking $10 million from the Virginia Department of Health Professions in return for 8 million allegedly stolen patient records. As reported in *Information Week*, the extortion note reads:

ATTENTION VIRGINIA I have your sh**! In *my* possession, right now, are 8,257,378 patient records and a total of 35,548,087 prescriptions. Also,

NEW DIRECTIONS FOR INSTITUTIONAL RESEARCH • DOI: 10.1002/ir

I made an encrypted backup and deleted the original. Unfortunately for Virginia, their backups seem to have gone missing, too. Uhoh :(" . . . "

If by the end of 7 days, you decide not to pony up, I'll go ahead and put this baby out on the market and accept the highest bid [Claburn, 2009].

Old Methods and New. Traditional application hacking techniques such as cross-site scripting and SQL injection together were 50 percent of application vulnerabilities in 2007 (Web Application Security Consortium [WASC], 2007) and continued to show wide use in 2008 (Internet Crime Complaint Center, 2008). Nevertheless, there is some evidence that hackers have become lazy and rely more on phishing and click-jacking techniques that trick the public into giving away what used to require work. That users continue to be gullible to trickery is illustrated by the continued success of an unrelated scam, the Nigerian Bank fraud letter. For the last four years (at least) Nigeria ranks among the top three countries from which fraud is perpetrated (Internet Crime Complaint Center, 2008). The gullibility of the public is even more apparent when we consider that Nigerian Bank fraud letters date back to the fax machine before the popularity of e-mail. Phishing scams are just one of many vulnerabilities discussed later in the chapter.

Old Regulations and New. Breach disclosure laws now present in forty-four states (National Conference of State Legislatures, 2009) add significantly to the average cost of a breach. One study done in 2007 estimates the cost at $197 for every record (Contos, 2009), which seems overstated. My personal experience was $40 per record for a breach of twenty-one thousand records where notification was by first-class mail, 50 percent of the addresses required research, and identity theft assistance was offered. Security professionals and colleagues from other universities have indicated costs in the range of $10 per record where e-mail notification is permitted. The problem with breach estimates is the wide variation of breach profiles and the difficulty of assigning a dollar value to lost reputation or, worse yet, lost revenue. For the purposes of this chapter, what is important to establish is that breach costs represent a nontrivial risk. Taking the low figure of $10 per record and the high figure of $197, let us say that the average breach of educational records will range from $210,000 to as high as $4 million from breach notification costs alone.

Old Habits. Thus far it has been shown that the increased number of security threats and their rising cost (including costs associated with breach notification laws) require that the information security function be complete and thorough. Yet diversity of governance patterns in both IR and information security creates information silos that increase the efforts of security programs and methodologies. There is no magic information security bullet; security programs require focused and thorough attention in the face of new and unprecedented losses. Old habits need to change.

The Human Factor

In this section I discuss security vulnerabilities that revolve around human behavior and for which a good security awareness program is the principal mitigation but for which technical mitigation may exist as well. The wisdom of a good security awareness program will become obvious as we proceed, as will the wisdom of those policy makers who wrote security awareness training requirements into various laws and standards.

The topics of this section all relate to data loss. We have long understood losing a data asset in a way that it is no longer recoverable; for this reason, regular backups are commonplace. But recent data breach notification laws emphasize a different dimension to the words *lost data*, that is, the sense in which data is exposed. In a data exposure, the entire data store remains intact, but some unauthorized person has obtained a copy of it. If a copy of our data store is lost or stolen in this way and it contains personally identifiable information (PII), the cost of breach cleanup will be significant. Earlier I noted the cost of an average data breach for educational institutions at $210,000 or higher. Thinking about this number with all those zeros helps us comprehend the risk we incur in handling it and invites us to compare our care for data assets with similar value.

How would you travel with $210,000 in cash? How would you carry it to the airport? Would you set the heavy titanium case of cash on the curb as you tipped the cab driver? Where would you put the cash while you ate lunch? Would you lock $210,000 in the back seat of your car? What would you do with the combination to the lock? Would you write it on a sticky note attached to the titanium case and leave both in the men's room or ladies' room? We will follow these questions in examining several threats involving the human factor.

Stolen Laptops and Other Portable Data Stores. These questions about cash invite us to reflect on the risk of carrying a laptop computer loaded with institutional data assets worth hundreds of thousands of dollars. If I wanted to have my laptop stolen, I would definitely carry it to the airport with me or lock it in plain sight on the back seat of my car. These are two of the places from which laptops are most commonly stolen. The existence of professional thieves at airports is not new, nor is the loss of property from a parked vehicle, nor is the laptop computer. What is relatively new is the rising number of professionals who travel with laptops and the capacity of disk drives to be loaded with institutional data. To put capacity in concrete terms, an ordinary laptop with a 120 GB drive will hold the entire enterprise database for an institution of twenty-five thousand students with ten years of history. This database would contain student records; financial aid; admission statistics; alumni giving records; and accounting, purchasing, and bursar records.

What is also relatively new is the targeting of laptops by thieves and some of their tactics. While traveling through an airport to a convention

Table 3.2. Top Twelve Thefts by Number Affected, 2008

Date	Institution	Number Affected	Device Stolen
4/17	University of Miami	2,100,000	Backup tape
6/10	University of Utah	1,500,000	Backup tape
5/1	Staten Island University Hospital	88,000	Desktop computer, backup hard drive
10/7	University of North Dakota	84,000	Laptop
6/6	Stanford University	72,000	Laptop
4/17	Multiple	40,379	Laptop
4/11	Cornell	40,000	Unstated
1/29	Georgetown	38,000	USB hard drive
4/16	Nippon Medical School	17,000	Portable computer
8/30	Rochester Institute of Technology, National Institute for the Deaf	13,800	Laptop
4/16	University of Virginia	7,000	Laptop
6/9	University of South Carolina	7,000	Computer

Source: Dodge (2009).

of educators, I witnessed the theft of a laptop belonging to an administrator at a neighboring university. The van driver carried one suitcase to the curb some twenty feet away, leaving the laptop in the van. As the administrator tipped the driver at the curb, a second van drove up and whisked away the laptop bag, recognized easily by its shape and size. In another common scenario, an executive paused at the ticket counter and set a laptop loaded with institutional data at his feet. It was gone when he turned around. Parked cars are also a risky place to leave laptops. Table 3.2 shows the vulnerability of educational laptops to theft. The reader who is unconvinced of this should Google the phrase "laptop stolen from car" and read the names of university, corporate, and military victims and the large number of records lost.

Laptop Passwords and the Need for Whole Disk Encryption. The university administrator whose laptop was hijacked from the van was distraught, as one might imagine, but he uttered words of hope: "My laptop had a password on it. That will protect my data, won't it?" Unfortunately, it was not protected. Windows, Macintosh, and other UNIX machines can be booted from a CD, making the data on the hard drive readily available without a password. Even commercial products that password-protect the hard drive may be bypassed by the manufacturer and presumably by hackers. None of these solutions would prevent an intruder from obtaining the data. Nor do these kinds of protection avoid the need to notify according to most state breach laws if data that could result in identity theft were on the drive.

So should we hire an armored truck to transport our laptops and portable data? There is an alternate solution. What can offer significant protection in the event of a lost laptop is whole-disk encryption using an industry standard encryption algorithm and an encryption key of satisfactory length. If the encryption algorithm is weak or the key too short, an intruder can decrypt the data. Instead of encrypting the whole disk, one could encrypt only the confidential files on the disk. That would be effective. However, the problem with encrypting only the relevant files on the disk is in knowing that one has identified all relevant files. Encrypting the whole disk avoids those nagging doubts following a breach: "Did I really put all confidential data files in the encrypted folder, or did I leave some of them unencrypted?"

Data breach notification laws vary from state to state. Most states say that if data is rendered unreadable (encrypted), notification in the event of breach is unnecessary. An occasional state may require breach notification of lost encrypted data; this explains the existence of odd-sounding notifications that go something like this: "We are sorry that we lost your social security number and credit card number; we are required by law to notify you; however, rest assured that your data was encrypted." Some states require that if you do business there and have a breach, you must notify breached residents of that state even if your institution is located in another state. This is particularly relevant in these days of distance learning where an institution may have offices in numerous states. Readers are urged to consult their institutional counsel on all matters of law.

PDAs, Music Players, Phones, and Memory Sticks. The risks associated with lost laptops are no less severe when the data is stored on other portable devices. Personal digital assistants (PDAs), music players, portable phones, and memory sticks (and various combinations) have all been used to store institutional data. Netbooks are the latest in this genre of device. What is new is the increased storage on these devices and their improved ability to receive and transmit data. Many music players have 160 GB hard drives, large enough to store the enterprise institutional database described earlier in this chapter. If these devices send and receive e-mail or browse the Web, it is inevitable that confidential institutional assets will find their way onto them and ultimately some device will be lost or stolen.

If an institution permits the circulation of reports through e-mail, large quantities of data will end up on portable devices that, if lost, could trigger the expense of a data breach notification. Who would have guessed that the true cost of the lost phone is $210,000 or more because it had a report containing social security numbers downloaded to it? Some portable devices such as the BlackBerry support data encryption, as do competing products. However, without a policy to the contrary, nothing prevents use of a device that supports Web mail, but does not support data encryption, from downloading toxic attachments. The unencrypted e-mail attachment could trigger the expense of a breach notification when the device is lost or stolen.

NEW DIRECTIONS FOR INSTITUTIONAL RESEARCH • DOI: 10.1002/ir

If these portable devices also support Web browsing, then a new set of concerns arises. Institutions that deliver reports through a Web browser should be concerned that reports containing toxic data could end up unencrypted on these devices undetected by the IR group that manages report distribution. Institutions should assess the risk of report distribution through e-mail or the Web, translate that risk into a dollar amount, and determine if it makes sense to enact controls. There are a number of possible strategic controls, but at minimum there should be a strategy.

One strategy would be to require encryption on all devices that receive institutional e-mail or browse confidential institutional data stores. BlackBerrys, iPhones, and Windows CE devices all support device encryption, though some devices in this genre do not. A second strategy would be to encrypt all reports that contain toxic data elements. Since not all portable devices support file decryption, this strategy would likely result in support of only a few. A third strategy would be to enact policies that restrict the kinds of devices that can access report stores over the Web; these could be supplemented by configuring browser parameters to enforce the policy. To prohibit handheld devices from Web browsing, configure the user agent string to permit only agent values equal to Internet Explorer or higher. The parameter is user configurable, so informed users could defeat the strategy. A fourth strategy would be to enact policies that restrict reports from being attached to e-mail.

E-mail to the Wrong Address. Only the second and fourth strategies mitigate data lost through e-mail attachments sent to the wrong recipient. It is easy to misaddress an e-mail. (Who has not had the type-ahead feature fill in an undesired result?) Although e-mail servers, transport, and storage may be properly encrypted, if an attachment is not, the damage may be uncorrectable once it is sent to the wrong address. Some e-mail services support retrieval of mail that has not been read, but this is small consolation if a confidential report is sent to the wrong distribution list.

Data Classification and Control. At this point it becomes apparent that toxic data such as social security numbers should be strictly controlled. These data elements should be eliminated from all reports that do not require them and from the reporting profiles of all users who do not need to report on them. Policies to this effect are a good start. Some technical solutions are effective and others less so. Data loss prevention tools that filter content leaving the organization can be intentionally bypassed by hackers using encryption or inadvertently by staff using a virtual private networking tunnel (also encrypted). Digital rights management strategies through which authorization rights travel with the file have been unreliable and unpopular (Shostack and Stewart, 2008). Some vendors offer vault-type products that log all access to critical data elements.

Passwords Weak and Strong. We rely on passwords to lock the door to our data assets, yet some passwords provide poor protection. If we inadvertently give our password to a hacker through a phishing scheme, it obviously provides no protection at all. IR professionals should make users aware that password cracking programs such as John the Ripper, readily available on the Web, are very effective at cracking weak passwords. (See Table 3.3, which is based on Alonso's statement that 50 percent of a 3 GHz processor can obtain 23.4 million hashes per second; Alonso, 2008.) Lucas (2009) also provides valuable insight into how long it takes to crack passwords. His alarming numbers are far more credible in 2010 in view of powerful computers built from as few as four over-the-counter computer graphic cards.

Cracking programs start by "guessing" a list of default passwords to databases and servers and then proceed to common dictionary words, followed by common words with a few numbers added to the end. These are all weak passwords that can be easily guessed. An eight-character password that uses at least one uppercase character, one lowercase character, a number, and one special character will slow these cracking programs significantly. A good password does not ensure that it will not be guessed; it only reduces the probabilities.

Password Hash Tables. More alarming than password guessing programs are tools that create and use databases of hashed passwords to look up a clear text password from the hash value. A hash value is like encryption, but it never gets decrypted. The hashed password is stored at creation time and compared to the password supplied and hashed at the time of authentication and log-in. Since the password stored and the password supplied were both hashed by the same hashing algorithm, they should match. Against these techniques, an eight-character password that uses uppercase, lowercase, numbers, and special characters will be more effective. This is because the hash database would need to contain all possible combinations (about 7.2 quadrillion) and has not yet been built in most cases. Some passwords used on the Windows operating system, however, can be an exception.

Against these techniques, an eight-character Windows password will not be effective if the "use LANMAN authorization" parameter is enabled. Effective passwords on Windows systems with the LANMAN parameter-enabled systems must have fifteen characters or more (Gates, 2009). What follows is an oversimplified explanation of why shorter Windows passwords may be vulnerable. Projects such as Rainbow Crack have made it possible to look up a clear text password given the known hash value. The Rainbow Crack project has produced databases of hash values for all possible combinations of a seven-character password using various algorithms including the LANMAN algorithm commonly used by Windows. In one column of these cracking databases are all possible clear text passwords of a given length, and in the other column is the corresponding hash value. Looking up the clear text password from its known hash value is a matter of a database query selecting on that hash value to retrieve the

Table 3.3. Password Recovery Speeds

Character Set Size	Password Length	Combinations	Combinations	Fast PC Attack: 3 GHz at 50 Percent	10 Fast PCs
62 (U, L, N)	6	57 billion	57,000,000,000	40 minutes	4 minutes
62	7	3.5 trillion	3,500,000,000,000	1.7 days	4.1 hours
62	8	218 trillion	218,000,000,000,000	107.6 days	10.7 days
94 (U, L, N, Special)	5	7.3 billion	7,339,000,000	5.2 minutes	31 seconds
94	6	690 billion	690,000,000,000	8.2 hours	49 minutes
94	7	64.8 trillion	64,847,000,000,000	32 days	3.2 days
94	8	6 quadrillion	6,095,000,000,000,000	8.2 years	301 days

Source: Calculated from Alonso (2008).

corresponding clear text value. Retrieval takes about five minutes against the 64 GB database—a database small enough to fit on today's personal computer.

The significance of LANMAN in this example is that Windows uses this algorithm for passwords that are fourteen characters or less. If the password is fifteen characters or more on Windows, the NTLM algorithm is used. LANMAN divides the fourteen-character password into two strings of seven characters and forces them into uppercase and uses no additional variables, called "seeds". The success of cracking a fourteen-character LANMAN password in a brief period of time is greater than .99 (Gates, 2009). Microsoft (2007) explains how to disable the LANMAN parameter forcing use of the NTLM encryption scheme.

Although LANMAN is an older algorithm and Windows supports newer alternatives, including NTLMv2 and Kerberos, the LANMAN vulnerability has current relevance because many shops leave the LANMAN compatibility flag on; otherwise, Windows 95/98 machines could not authenticate natively. By leaving this flag on, the vulnerability described here is created even though non-Windows 95/98 log-ins may use NTLMv2 to authenticate to the same server. It is the existence of the LANMAN password file on the server that results in the vulnerability.

Password vulnerabilities are compounded whenever each user on a system has access to read the password database. Thus, a single guessed password exposes the whole password database to cracking techniques. Even when the password database may be read only by accounts having administrator rights, there is vulnerability for organizations that grant administrator rights to ordinary user accounts with weak passwords and also put the same administrator account or password on every machine. The hacker gains access to the weak account through which the whole password file is exposed and through which the administrator account on every machine in the organization containing it is also exposed. Current versions of most operating systems mitigate the risk of password file exposure by use of a shadow file that older versions do not use.

These vulnerabilities point to the need for strong passwords that are changed frequently—every ninety days. The password policy required by the Payment Card Industry Data Security Standard is a good one to follow. More important is the need to recognize the inherent weakness of passwords and the need to deploy two-factor authentication. Two-factor authentication asks for two forms of authentication, such as something you know (a password) and something you have (such as a random number generated by a pocket-sized hardware token).

Other common methods of obtaining passwords are phishing, social engineering, keystroke logging, wiretapping, log-in spoofing, shoulder surfing, and dumpster diving. Shoulder surfing and dumpster diving require the perpetrator to be physically near the institution, which is not a common pattern for data educational data exposures. Keystroke loggers (a form of Trojan horse) or phishing (where you are tricked by a request for your password) are more likely ways that the IR professional could lose data. Phishing requires that the victim fall for some request such as, "The help desk is updating its record. Enter your username and password here, or you will be locked out for a hundred years." Such requests are certainly below the dignity of the average IR professional. Keystroke loggers seem far more likely to nab the typical IR professional. But how does one get infected by a keystroke logger? Infection commonly occurs by clicking on some Web page that will download the executable "needed to display the Halloween card a secret admirer sent you" or some similar scam. More recent "click jacking" scams layer a fake screen over a legitimate one such as a password reset screen and line the fields up appropriately. Virus and malware protection may be of some help in defeating the keystroke logger, but signatures used by detection software have been recently faked. The details of these password scams are ever changing, but the common factor in most of them is all of us: the human factor. The risk of breaches caused by disgruntled employees has been described well in two articles supplied by Cisco Systems (2008a and 2008b) as well as RSA (2008).

Vulnerabilities from the human factor require a good security awareness program that continually reinforces circumspect computer practices.

The Application

General Vulnerabilities. Software applications are commonly distinguished from the servers and networks on which they run. Software applications that are widely used by IR professionals include query and reporting tools, statistical analysis packages, databases, Web applications, and software Web servers like Apache. Some security principles are shared by software applications and their hardware server infrastructure. For example, an FBI report indicates that 99 percent of security intrusions are from known vulnerabilities or configuration errors (Hamelin, 2009). These include hardware as well as application software vulnerabilities. Given that such a large percentage of intrusions are from known issues, why not make a list of these vulnerabilities, check data centers for their existence, and fix the vulnerability before an intrusion occurs? Even if the percentage were 49 instead of 99, this action would seem to be required.

In fact, a genre of software does exist to scan a data center against lists of known vulnerabilities (vulnerability scan) or attempt to penetrate the vulnerability (penetration test), and many organizations run such software on a regular basis. Many data centers run free vulnerability scanning and penetration testing tools such as Nessus or Core Impact; others pay vendors to run more costly equivalents. Since new vulnerabilities are discovered daily, a whole industry has sprung up to research them and build discovery into these automated tools. Whether one runs the free versions or the more costly commercial versions depends on an organization's risk tolerance and how quickly newly discovered vulnerabilities make it to the known list used by your favorite vulnerability scanning software. The earlier statement that 99 percent of intrusions come from vulnerabilities and configuration errors that are known contains an implied irony: that many data centers are obviously not doing basic vulnerability scanning or not acting to fix the results.

Even more ironic is that as far back as 2002, Congress saw the importance of having current vulnerability lists and mandated that such lists be built and that selected federal computer resources be checked against them (National Institute of Standards and Technology, 2009). This mandate resulted in the National Vulnerability Database (NVD) for automating vulnerability management, security measurement, and compliance checking from National Institute of Standards and Technology (NIST). The project was sponsored by the Department of Homeland Security (DHS) National Cyber Security Division/US-CERT. Its 142 vulnerability checklists covering seventy-nine products are used for vulnerability assessment programs.

A second security principle that applies to both applications and the server infrastructure on which they run is that 90 percent of breaches involve either a system unknown to the organization or a system storing data the organization did not know existed (Contos, 2009). Implied in this statistic is that known resources have better security protection than unknown ones, an obvious finding that begs to be elaborated. The focus appears to be on who knows about these resources. Obviously someone knew about them at one time or perhaps still knows about them. But did the security function know about them? The real lesson is that resources get better security protection when those charged with information security know that the resources exist. That raises a further question for IR professionals: Do the information security professionals in your organization know about IR data assets so as to protect them? If not, does IR accept full responsibility to secure them? Perhaps the security responsibilities are split. These questions raise again the importance of clear information security governance. The immediate action to take concerning unknown assets is to be sure that security governance of them is clearly defined and that the office responsible includes them in institutional protections, penetration tests, and audits.

Application-Specific Vulnerabilities. Regarding breaches that occur through the application as opposed to the hardware or the network, one expert has placed this number at greater than 80 percent of the total (Cole, 2006; Cole and Ring, 2006). It is difficult to get good statistics that classify vulnerabilities by type because much of the research is funded by vendors (Shostack and Stewart, 2008) but also because breach classification and typology is in an immature stage. However, if Cole and other researchers are only half right, significant attention must be paid to the application as a source of vulnerability.

Maturity of Application Vulnerability Classification. Recent efforts have been made to identify and classify vulnerabilities in a way that produces reliable statistics and promotes research that ultimately reduces them. One organization that promotes application security is the Open Web Application Security Project (OWASP). It lists 162 vulnerabilities such as buffer overflow, insecure temporary file, and memory leak and 57 attack techniques that attackers use to exploit vulnerabilities. OWASP also publishes a running list of the top ten application vulnerabilities—the OWASP Top Ten Project (OWASP, 2007). The U.S. Federal Trade Commission, U.S. Defense Information Systems Agency, and the Payment Card Industry Data Security Standard all endorse use of the OWASP Top Ten in one way or another.

Two of the top vulnerabilities listed on the OWASP Top Ten are cross-site scripting (XSS) and injection flaws, particularly SQL injection. SQL injection vulnerabilities occur whenever an application sends user-supplied data to a Web server without first validating the input. At the end of a Web input string could be an SQL statement that essentially says to the database, "Give me every record, including all the confidential stuff." Like SQL injection, cross-site scripting is a vulnerability that occurs because of coding weaknesses in the Web applications that one visits through a Web browser. With cross-site scripting, the browser has no way of distinguishing code that has been planted on the Web site by the hacker from legitimate code, so it executes all of it. Bad results include sending the user's cookie to the hacker, who uses the cookie to hijack the session and do further damage.

WASC is a second group that promotes application security research, including open source program code and best-practice security standards. WASC also highlights vulnerabilities from cross-site scripting and SQL injection, showing in 2007 that 41 percent of breaches resulted from the former and 9 percent from the latter (WASC, 2007). One vendor reports that over 20 percent of breaches resulted from SQL injection (Breach Security Labs, 2007). Web pages poorly written and poorly secured risk database compromise through password exposure.

The Common Vulnerability Exposure (CVE) project is a third project that has contributed significantly to accurate vulnerability classification and breach reporting. CVE is a dictionary of publicly known information security vulnerabilities, a project sponsored by the National Cyber Security Division of the U.S. Department of Homeland Security. CVE identifiers (such as "CVE-1999–0067") are accompanied by a brief description of the security vulnerability or exposure and any pertinent references to vulnerability reports and advisories called OVAL-IDs. CVE identifiers are used by information security product and service vendors and researchers as a standard method for identifying vulnerabilities and for cross-linking with other repositories that also use CVE identifiers ("Common Vulnerabilities and Exposures," 2009).

Vulnerability Scanning. The importance of projects like CVE, WASC, and OWASP is that they make possible and promote vulnerability scanning tools. Remember that most data breaches occur through known vulnerabilities that could have been detected by vulnerability scanning tools before the breach occurred. The leading causes of data breach, such as cross-site scripting and SQL injection, as well as hundreds of others, therefore, can be detected before they are exploited. Vulnerability testing should be done against vendor-supplied products as well as home-grown applications.

Reporting Tools With Pass-Through Accounts. Institutional research reporting environments have rich data stores, with a wide variety of data elements in large quantities. Moreover, IR professionals must manage data access for a large number of people across the institution that need to access the data store. Finally, many commercial tools do not use native database security but rely on their own security and access methods. To do this, they typically require a database account known as a pass-through account. It might well be called the "read anything in the world account" or possibly even the "disaster is looming around the corner" account. If the pass-through account is compromised by an intruder, all of the data is retrievable. Individuals in the organization may also have a read-all account, but vendor pass-through accounts are unique in that the account name and the default password are in hacker databases around the world. Software upgrades may even reset the password on these accounts to their defaults. Vulnerability testing will likely discover these disasters ready to happen. If one is in the market for a new reporting tool, one might question the wisdom of a vendor who would choose to use a database pass-through account, and consequently write a proprietary access control mechanism, rather than use native and more widely tested access control mechanisms written by the database vendor.

The Server Infrastructure

Network security is beyond the scope of this chapter, and comments on securing the server infrastructure will be brief and high level, primarily because most IR professionals touch these areas least; also, most breaches are at the application level. (For more information on these topics, see Harris, 2007; Tipton and Henry, 2007; Tipton and Krause, 2008; and Hansche, Berti, and Hare, 2004.)

Nevertheless, some basic infrastructure security principles must not go unstated. We must protect servers housing confidential data using multiple layers of protection that include several firewalls and server hardening. We must run hardening software that verifies server parameters before a server is put into production and after significant changes; for example, Microsoft Baseline Security Analyzer (MSBA). Knowing that 99 percent of intrusions are from known vulnerabilities or configuration errors (Hamelin, 2009), we must apply patches promptly and run vulnerability scans and penetration tests. In spite of its weaknesses, we must run virus protection software and update the signature file daily. We must deploy host-based intrusion detection.

We must encrypt backup tapes, and portable media such as USB drives used by technical staff, recognizing that 73.8 percent of educational records lost or stolen in 2008 resulted from stolen media.

We must make an inventory of servers and data stores and send the inventory to the chief information security officer or the person holding that function. We must remember that 90 percent of breaches involve either a system unknown to the organization or a system storing data the organization did not know existed (Contos, 2009).

We must use strong passwords and require them to be changed every ninety days. We must also recognize the inherent weakness of passwords and deploy two-factor authentication, which could include a password plus a pocket-sized hardware token with time-synched seed numbers. For a summary of vulnerability and mitigation refer to Table 3.4.

Table 3.4. Summary of Vulnerability and Mitigation

Vulnerability	Associated Evidence	Mitigation
Lost or stolen laptops or USB devices	Common	Whole disk encryption
E-mail report to wrong location		Encryption or policy
Weak passwords	See Table 3.3	Two-factor or better passwords
Phishing	Increased on federal report	Security awareness program
Breach reporting costs	44 states	Security plan or risk assessment
Known vulnerabilities	99% of breached assets	Vulnerability scan
Assets unknown to security management	90% of breached assets	Clear governance of assets
Application breaches	80% of breaches	Vulnerability scan
SQL injection	9% to 20% of application breaches	Vulnerability scan
Cross-site scripting	41% of application breaches	Security awareness program
Develop poor applications		OWASP standards or scan
Lost or stolen backup tapes	73.3% of lost education records	Encrypt backup tapes
Poor server configuration		Hardening guides or vulnerability scan
No security program or policy	Violation of GLBA/PCI	Security plan or risk assessment

Information Security Governance and the Security Plan

Given the risk implied in this sampling of threats to institutional data assets, the security of these assets must be well managed and thorough. Proper management implies a security plan that is complete, well understood, based on risk, and properly governed through established channels that are accountable to the executive level. But what is an information security plan, how is it established, and how is it governed?

An information security plan or program is a concise statement of the security actions to be taken by an organization. It generally includes the risk that the action is intended to mitigate, the person responsible for each action, the estimated cost, and the success metrics. An information security plan may be strategic, brief, and directed to governing boards and executive management, or it may be operational, detailed, and directed toward middle management and implementation teams. Both types of plan are needed, with the strategic plan preceding the operational plan.

Information Security Governance. Before an information security plan may be written, a framework of information security governance must be established. Much failure of the information security function has occurred because information security governance was created impulsively, with little thought, often in reaction to some breach and with little access to executive management. Silos of information security practice that impede or defeat a complete set of security functions and agile response may result if governance is haphazard. So important is information security governance to security success that the International Standards Organization (ISO) has established a certification in security governance for organizations. The certification is built around the ISO 27003 standard. Also indicative of the importance of information security governance is the work done by a congressional committee.

Accountability to Governing Board. What does good information security governance look like? In 2004 the Best Practices and Metrics Team of the Corporate Information Security Working Group (CISWG) convened by U.S. Representative Adam Putnam (R-Florida) answered this question. This group, including representatives from Educause, refined a document called "Information Security Program Elements" and developed metrics to support each of the elements. They recommended that educational institutions make the information security function concrete by adopting a policy statement something like the following (CISWG, 2004):

In order to promote the security mandate of the university, (fill in some governing body) shall:

NEW DIRECTIONS FOR INSTITUTIONAL RESEARCH • DOI: 10.1002/ir

1. Oversee risk management and compliance programs pertaining to information security such as Sarbanes-Oxley, HIPAA, Gramm-Leach-Bliley, and PCI.
2. Approve and adopt broad information security program principles and approve assignment of key managers responsible for information security.
3. Strive to protect the interests of all stakeholders dependent on information security.
4. Review information security policies regarding strategic partners and other third-parties.
5. Strive to ensure business continuity.
6. Review provisions for internal and external audits of the information security program.
7. Collaborate with management to specify the information security metrics to be reported to the board.

Information Security Coordination. In addition to high-level principles of governance, the CISWG also spoke to the question of information security coordination or management by recommending that institutions adopt a statement something like the following:

In order to promote the security mandate of the university, management shall:
1. Establish information security management policies and controls and monitor compliance.
2. Assign information security roles, responsibilities, required skills, and enforce role-base information access privileges.
3. Assess information risks, establish risk thresholds and actively manage risk mitigation.
4. Ensure implementation of information security requirements for strategic partners and other third-parties.
5. Identify and classify information assets.
6. Implement and test business continuity plans.
7. Approve information systems architecture during acquisition, development, operations, and maintenance.
8. Protect the physical environment.
9. Ensure internal and external audits of the information security program with timely follow-up.
10. Collaborate with security staff to specify the information security metrics to be reported to management.

Qualified Security Leadership. The information security coordination and accountability described here call for qualified security leadership. But what constitutes a qualified security professional? Security challenges to information assets spawned certifications some fifteen years ago, and new ones continue to emerge each year. The Global Information Assurance Certification (GIAC) is affiliated with the SANS Institute, which describes itself as the most trusted and the largest source for information security training, certification, and research in the world. However, the Certified Information Systems Security Professional (CISSP) is perhaps the first and most highly sought after certification for the information security professional. Offered by the International Information Systems Security Consortium (ISC2), its examination is often described as "a mile wide and an inch deep." As such it covers not only technical details but also a high level perspective on risk and governance that is sometimes missed completely by those who come from technical backgrounds. Organizations of security professionals such as the Information Systems Security Association (ISSA) can help organizations find qualified security leadership.

Erickson and Howard (2007) echo the importance of information security governance, in their finding that organizational mismanagement plays a large role in data breaches.

The Security Plan. After an organization has established its information security governance and coordination pattern, including who has the role of chief information security officer (CISO), the CISO should lead the creation of an information security plan (sometimes called a program) based on a risk assessment of known information assets. Once the organization has identified its primary information security risks, the CISO should help the organization attach a general cost to the mitigation of each risk and lead those with budget authority to prioritize the risk mitigation. The security risk mitigation strategy is then expanded into an operational security plan.

Strategic (high-level) security plans prioritize a list of security initiatives to the governing boards and executive management for the next three to five years. Operational (lower-level) security plans outline significant details for the upcoming twelve to eighteen months and are addressed to the middle management and operational teams. The security plan in a given year will not likely address all known risk or necessarily be balanced by addressing a full domain set of information security concerns. It addresses whatever the institution thinks is its greatest risks. The plan will propose a mitigation strategy for each risk identified and an approximate cost, state who will lead the effort, and give metrics of success. Simple examples of mitigation strategies are to purchase a firewall, contract for intrusion detection, build a security awareness program, or implement a password policy. Each of these examples imposes a control over the identified risk.

Information security plans need to match institutional priorities, staffing levels, the budget, and risk tolerance. These plans are the basis by

which governing boards and executives are given the opportunity to mitigate risk by funding the plan or, alternately, accept the risk themselves by
not funding the plan. Without an information security plan, known risk
may never rise to the attention of the executive level and instead be inadvertently and inappropriately accepted at a level of the organization that
is too low. Information security plans are part of an overall information
management plan.

Formal Risk Assessment. An information security plan should be
based on a risk assessment of known assets. This strategy will help prioritize security initiatives and permit risk to be communicated to and
addressed at the executive level, where the institutional risk tolerance policy, formal or informal, can be applied to it. The difficulties in any risk
assessment are in knowing that all assets have been identified and that the
significant threats to those assets have been identified. The risk assessment is only as complete as the list of assets and threats. The last step is
estimating the likelihood that a threat will become an actual exposure.
This last step may prove to be the most difficult of all.

Asset identification may begin with inventories but will likely involve
a variety of inputs from staff. Begin with the data stores. As a model, it will
be helpful to obtain an asset list that another institution has built for this
purpose.

Identification of threats should be systematic and thorough, treating
all categories of the information security common body of knowledge
(Tipton and Henry, 2007) and using known standards such as the ISO
27002. The goal is the complete set of security functions alluded to at the
beginning of this chapter. What good is it to put a super lock on the front
door of your house if the back door and windows are wide open? Or to
what effect does one put a 24-character password on a server if the server
may be easily stolen from a room whose door is never locked? A complete
set of security functions includes not only good passwords and application
security but all other domains or standards, such as the information security common body of knowledge and the ISO 27002. The application and
server vulnerability lists from OSWASP, CVE, and the WASC project elaborated earlier in this chapter help achieve a complete set of security functions as well. Advanced threat list seekers may find the Microsoft (2009)
material on threat modeling helpful.

The final step in risk assessment, estimating the likelihood that a
threat will become actual, exposes the limitation of the quantitative risk
methodology for information security; this limitation will force us to more
qualitative methods. In the financial sector, risk assessment is a mature
methodology that has been applied for over a hundred years. In this sector
we have reliable statistics in the form of actuarial tables that provide probabilities of various events. Risk assessment is also significantly developed
in the area of physical security, where emergency response teams and law
enforcement have contributed. But in the area of information technology,

risk assessment is a relatively new and somewhat immature discipline. Quantitative approaches seem simple enough on the surface, but most fail for lack of reliable exposure statistics. For example, the following formula seems simple enough:

$$(\text{Asset value} \times \text{exposure factor} = \text{Single loss exposure})$$
$$\times \text{ annualized rate of occurrence}$$
$$= \text{Annualized loss expectancy}$$

However, when one attempts to assign an exposure factor to even the simplest of information technology threats, it becomes apparent how difficult these quantitative approaches can be given the current stage of information security practice. No actuarial tables exist.

Qualitative Risk Assessment. A number of qualitative approaches to risk assessment such as OCTAVE, OCTAVE light, and STAR are available and in use, but these can be cumbersome and time intensive, especially for smaller institutions. Their value for the time spent is in the institutional awareness they create by getting technical staff and administrators to contribute. One simple alternative to these longer methodologies is the risk assessment tool provided by Educause (2009). Another simple strategy is to verify an institution's security plan against that of another institution known to have done risk assessment; a kind of risk assessment in reverse.

Risk assessment based on qualitative interviews has definite pitfalls. If the institution has had a recent breach, the risk climate produced by it could result in most security resources spent on yesterday's breach or the breach of a neighboring institution. Perceived risk has a subjective element that is difficult to overcome. Shostack and Stewart (2008) illustrate this well for the inquiring mind. Risk assessment tools attempt to minimize subjective risk evaluation in the allocation of resources to the security plan. Quantitative risk assessment would be superior if actuarial tables of information security risk existed, but since they do not, these qualitative methods are currently the best available.

Complete Set of Security Functions. Security functions are any of the activities and instruments that go into securing the enterprise. A complete set of security functions should address all domains of information security risk. We have seen that risk assessment must take into consideration a complete set of security threats. Information security controls such as policy should be enacted, but controls should not be enacted arbitrarily but only to mitigate risk that the organization does not wish to tolerate.

A variety of information security standards are available that lead to a complete set of security functions, or at least attempt to do so. I have noted the ISO/IEC 27002 with its twelve major categories:

- Security policy
- Organizational security
- Asset classification
- Personnel security
- Physical and environmental security
- Communications and operations management
- Access control
- System development and maintenance
- Business continuity management
- Compliance
- Incident management
- Security plans

I have noted as well the ten domains of the Common Body of Knowledge. To this I might add the domains of the National Institute of Standards (NIST). The topics of the SANS Institute and the ITIL security standards both rely on ISO/IEC 27002.

Clear assignment of each element of a set of security functions that is complete is more significant than the exact security governance structure. Security functions may be distributed across various and (even chaotic) management and governance structures and still be effective. Diversity of governance standards can result in information silos that defeat good information security, but it need not. A security plan based on recurring risk assessment against industry standards and regular audits will go a long way to defeat organizational information silos and governance issues.

Information security plans are generally based on known standards such as the ISO/IEC 27000 (17799) series standards, or the topics of the SANS Institute, or the domains of ISC2, or the elements of NIST or of PCI. If so, the organization may evaluate risk associated with each element of the standard and prioritize selected standards to be addressed that year or in an eighteen-month initiative. The overall goal could be compliance with all elements of the standard within a time period such as five years.

Controls That Mitigate Risk. A variety of mitigation controls have been mentioned already. Information security policy is an additional kind of control that can mitigate risk. However, security policy is often developed as a result of some organizational crisis rather than as a matter of long-term strategy. One savant has said that for some institutions, the history of their security incidents may be read by examining the history of their policy development. In contrast to this squeaky wheel approach, security policy should be developed intentionally as part of an overall security plan. Examples of security policy are available through Educause (2009).

Conclusion

We have observed that information security threats to educational institutions and their data assets have worsened significantly over the past few years. Traditional threats through the human factor, the application, and the server infrastructure have grown in both variety and consequence. A stolen laptop no longer contains only a few grade files and social security numbers but tens or even hundreds of thousands of toxic assets. Vulnerabilities to Web and database tools and the applications built on them are discovered almost daily and require prompt patching and professional programming. These vulnerabilities can sabotage an entire database in a matter of hours if left unattended. Even the server infrastructure and networks into which so many resources have been poured and from which we might expect stability must be viewed as living, breathing organisms that require the systematic attention of professionals.

To these threats have been added new consequences. The rich data stores of institutional research have been discovered and targeted by petty (but systematic) thieves and organized crime. With the skill of a good institutional research professional, these opportunists harvest the results of multiple breaches into databases of full identity profiles for sale and profit. Even when breached data does not wind up in the hands of professional thieves, new disclosure laws create financial liabilities for even a small educational institution.

To address this rapidly developing threat, the flexible and informal management structures of the academy that have led to innovation and rapid change must be supplemented by a systematic information security plan based on risk assessment and sanctioned at the executive level. This security plan must ensure that all security functions, as measured by some accepted standard, are present within the organization regardless of its structure. Resources must be allocated to these tasks in an operational security plan. The decision to fund the strategic and operational security plans must be at the executive level, where the risk is also communicated and accepted. Security policy, standards, and procedures must be put in place, communicated, and audited for compliance. In short, the response to the new threats must complete, involving all security functions, must be timely, must be measured, and must be based on risk assessment.

References

Alonso, F. O. "The Extinction of Password Authentication." *ISSA Journal*, 2008, 6, 29–32.

Breach Security Labs. "Breach Security Labs Publishes Report on Significant Web Hacking Incidents in 2007: Government, Social Networking and Web Hosting Providers Among the Most Frequently Compromised Websites; Nearly 70 Percent Financially Motivated." 2007. Retrieved May 13, 2010, from http://www.breach

.com/news-events/press-releases/breach-security-labs-publishes-report-on-significant-web-hacking-incidents-in-2007.html.

Brenner, S. W. *Cyberthreats: The Emerging Faultlines of the Nation State.* New York: Oxford University Press, 2009.

Carr, J. "Finjan: Chinese Cybercrime Networks Fill Void Left By Russian Business Network." *Security Magazine*, Dec. 18, 2008. Retrieved May 13, 2010, from http://www.scmagazineus.com/Finjan-Chinese-cybercrime-networks-fill-void-left-by-Russian-Business-Network/article/100002/.

Cisco Systems. "Data Leakage Worldwide: The High Cost of Insider Threats." Cisco Systems, 2008a. Retrieved May 10, 2010, from http://www.cisco.com/en/US/solutions/collateral/ns170/ns896/ns895/white_paper_c11–506224.pdf.

Cisco Systems. "Data Leakage Worldwide: The Effectiveness of Security Policies." Cisco Systems. 2008b. Retrieved May 10, 2010, from http://www.cisco.com/en/US/solutions/collateral/ns170/ns896/ns895/white_paper_c11–503131.html.

Claburn, T. "Virginia Health Data Potentially Held Hostage." *InformationWeek*, May 4, 2009. Retrieved May 13, 2010, from http://www.informationweek.com/news/security/attacks/showArticle.jhtml?articleID=217201397&subSection=Attacks/breaches.

Cole, E. "Keynote Address: Question and Answer Session." Cisco Evil Insider Conference, Cincinnati, Ohio, 2006.

Cole, E., and Ring, S. *Insider Threat: Protecting the Enterprise from Sabotage, Spying, and Theft.* Rockland, Mass.: Syngress Publishing, 2006.

"Common Vulnerabilities and Exposures." Sponsored by the Department of Homeland Security (DHS) National Cyber Security Division. 2009. Retrieved May 10, 2010, from http://cve.mitre.org/.

Contos, B. "Keynote Address." CADRE Security Conference and Expo 2009. Sharonville Conference Center, Cincinnati, Ohio, 2009.

Corporate Information Security Working Group (CISWG). "Information Security Program Elements." 2004. www.educause.edu/ir/library/word/SWR0514.doc.

Dodge, A. "Educational Security Incidents (ESI) Year in Review 2008." 2009. Retrieved May 13, 2010, from http://www.adamdodge.com/esi/year_review_2008.

Educause. "IT Security Guide." 2009. Retrieved May 10, 2009, from https://wiki.internet2.edu/confluence/display/secguide/Home.

Erickson, K., and Howard, P. N. "A Case of Mistaken Identity? News Accounts of Hacker, Consumer, and Organizational Responsibility for Compromised Digital Records." *Journal of Computer-Mediated Communication*, 2007, *12*. Retrieved May 10, 2010, from http://jcmc.indiana.edu/vol12/issue4/.

Gates, C. "Tutorial: Rainbow Tables and Rainbow Crack." 2009. Retrieved May 13, 2010, from http://www.ethicalhacker.net/content/view/94/24/.

Goggans, C. "Russian Mafia Is Largest Cyber Crime Syndicate." *Times of India*, Dec. 7, 2008. Retrieved May 13, 2010, from http://timesofindia.indiatimes.com/Pune/Russian_mafia_is_largest_cyber_crime_syndicate/articleshow/3803018.cms.

Hamelin, M. "Keynote Address." CADRE Security Conference and Expo 2009, Cincinnati, Ohio, 2009.

Hansche, S., Berti, J., and Hare, C. *Official (ISC)2 Guide to the CISSP Exam.* Boca Raton, Fla.: Auerbach Publications, 2004.

Harris, S. *CISSP Certification All-in-One Exam Guide.* (4th ed.) New York: McGraw-Hill, 2007.

Internet Crime Complaint Center. "2008 Internet Crime Report." 2008. Retrieved May 13, 2010, from http://www.ic3.gov/media/annualreports.aspx.

Lucas, I. "Password Recovery Speeds: How Long Will Your Password Stand Up?" 2009. Retrieved May 13, 2010, from http://www.lockdown.co.uk/?pg=combi.

Mayer, A. "Security Risk and Overcoming IT Silos." *ISSA Journal*, 2008, *6*(12), 10–12.

Microsoft. "How to Enable NTLM v2 Authentication." 2007. Retrieved May 13, 2010, from http://support.microsoft.com/kb/239869.

Microsoft. "Security Guidance and Threat Modeling." Microsoft Threat Modeling Blog, July 2009. Retrieved May 13, 2010, from http://blogs.msdn.com/threatmodeling/.

Naraine, R. "Cybercrime More Widespread, Skillful, Dangerous Than Ever." *FoxNews.com/E-Week.com*, April 13, 2006. Retrieved May 13, 2010, from http://www.foxnews.com/story/0,2933,191375,00.html.

National Conference of State Legislatures. "State Security Breach Notification Laws as of April 12, 2010." 2009. Retrieved May 13, 2010, from http://www.ncsl.org/IssuesResearch/TelecommunicationsInformationTechnology/SecurityBreachNotificationLaws/tabid/13489/Default.aspx.

National Institute of Standards and Technology. "National Vulnerability Database (NVD): For Automating Vulnerability Management, Security Measurement, and Compliance Checking." Sponsored by the Department of Homeland Security National Cyber Security Division/US-CERT. 2009. Retrieved May 13, 2010, from http://checklists.nist.gov/.

Open Web Application Security Project (OWASP). "OWASP Top Ten Project." 2007. Retrieved May 10, 2009, from http://www.owasp.org/index.php/Category:OWASP_Top_Ten_Project.

RSA. "The 2008 Insider Threat Survey." 2008. Retrieved May 13, 2010, from http://www.rsa.com/press_release.aspx?id=9703.

Shostack, A., and Stewart, A. *The New School of Information Security.* Reading, Mass.: Addison-Wesley, 2008.

Tipton, H. F., and Henry, K. *Official (ISC)2 Guide to the CISSP CBK.* Boca Raton, Fla.: Auerbach Publications, 2007.

Tipton, H. F., and Krause, M. *Information Security Management Handbook.* (6th ed.) Boca Raton, Fla.: Auerbach Publications, 2008.

Web Application Security Consortium (WASC). "WASC Web Application Security Statistics Project 2007." 2007. Retrieved May 13, 2010, from http://www.net-security.org/secworld.php?id=6501.

WILLIAM L. CUSTER *is the information security policy manager for Miami University in Oxford, Ohio.*

This chapter addresses the issue of higher education institution policies and procedures in regard to background checks for students, staff, and faculty in light of homeland security concerns.

Homeland Security Initiatives and Background Checks in Higher Education

Stephanie Hughes, Eileen Weisenbach Keller, Giles T. Hertz

In recent years, colleges and universities have faced a new challenge. While there has been a movement underway on college campuses to increase the safety of a wide range of university constituents through criminal background checks (CBCs), in most cases this movement has failed to include CBCs of foreign faculty and student populations. The arguments given for why universities do not incorporate international criminal background checks on foreign employees and students include cost, limited access, the accuracy and timeliness of these checks, and an assumption that the check has already been conducted by the U.S. government, before the person entered the country.

Despite stronger federal legislation aimed at bolstering homeland security initiatives for college campuses, there is still no federal requirement for universities to conduct CBCs on foreign employees or students arriving in the United States to work or attend colleges and universities. For example, the existing visa process requires a CBC in only two cases: where a hit appears when the applicant's name is run against the Consular Lookout and Support System's (CLASS) database to identify known terrorists and where the applicant has self-disclosed a criminal, mental health, or terrorism history. Even the USA PATRIOT Act (Patriot Act), a federal law passed in the aftermath of the terrorist attacks of 2001 and designed to intercept and obstruct terrorist activities, does not mandate background checks on foreign nationals attending U.S. colleges and

New Directions for Institutional Research, no. 146, Summer 2010 © Wiley Periodicals, Inc.
Published online in Wiley InterScience (www.interscience.wiley.com) • DOI: 10.1002/ir.342

universities. It does designate the use of the Student and Exchange Visitor Information System (SEVIS) to track foreign visitors and more easily access and monitor electronic communication patterns of individuals suspected of engaging in terrorist activities. By comparison, the Public Health Security and Bioterrorism Preparedness and Response Act of 2002 outlines a procedure for requiring a CBC of a foreign national. However, under this law, only individuals who will be working in university laboratories with particular biological agents will be required to register with the federal government and undergo a security risk assessment (Catholic University, 2008). This law applies to both domestic and foreign employees, and checks are conducted by the federal government through the office of the U.S. attorney general. Individual state legislatures, possibly recognizing the inadequacy of federal legislation, have pushed through their own laws mandating background checks on all newly hired employees working at state-supported institutions, and these laws sometimes include CBCs on foreign nationals.

The underutilization of CBCs on foreign students and employees exists despite record-high levels of foreign students coming to study at U.S. universities. More than 620,000 international students enrolled in U.S. colleges and universities for the 2007–2008 academic year, a 7 percent increase over the 2006–2007 academic year (Maslen, 2008). Increased legislation and security-enhanced visa processes would seem to be designed to manage this influx of foreign students, but closer examination highlights continuing security gaps. These gaps exist despite analysis that showed a number of the 9/11 terrorists had entered the United States through either visitor or student visa channels.

Institutional planning and research offices could help lead the way on policy development in this area given that they are responsible for providing university administrators and top management with information that supports institutional planning, policy formation, and decision making. These offices could help administrators by providing specific detail on overall numbers of foreign students, student compliance with SEVIS, and numbers of foreign employees and students employed on college campuses and across all colleges and universities. This would provide a much more robust picture of the issues associated with this topic and facilitate movement toward a more comprehensive approach to managing and mitigating this risk.

Crime and the Criminal Background Check Process

U.S. employers' use of CBCs to mitigate the potential risk posed by personnel has increased dramatically over the past decade. In a 2005 survey conducted by the Society for Human Resource Management (SHRM), 80 percent of employers surveyed indicated that they now conduct CBCs, up from 51 percent in 1996 (Gardner, 2008). This increase has coincided with an increased number of people who have been incarcerated, with an estimated 7.3 million adults held under correctional supervision (covering probation, jail, prison, or parole) in 2007, up from an estimated 1.8 million in 1980 (U.S. Department of Justice Statistics, 2007). As these numbers have increased, so has the interest in conducting CBCs. Increasingly evidence of the use of CBCs across different industries and in both public and private domains continues to emerge. Connerly, Arvey, and Bernardy (2001) evaluated local governments' use of CBCs as a way to reduce risk during the hiring process. All of the groups reported using CBCs on at least some employees. Nevertheless, there remained significant gaps in the use of CBCs across all employee groups, with only 50 percent indicating that they do CBCs on all prospective employees. These findings suggest that while the use of checks is commonplace in municipal settings, the less-than-comprehensive application of these checks leaves reason to doubt their impact on reducing the risk of unknowingly hiring criminal offenders (Hughes, Hertz, and White, 2009).

While these studies suggest that the use of CBCs is increasing within and across different environments, the effectiveness of CBCs at reducing an organization's risk and subsequent liability remains underexamined. Some articles provide anecdotal examples of organizations that have exposed themselves to increased liability by failing to learn about prior criminal convictions associated with employees in their organizations. Supporting these anecdotal examples, several studies have shown that recidivism rates among ex-prisoners are high (Langan and Levine, 2002; Kurlychek, Brame, and Bushway, 2006; Gendreau, Little, and Goggin, 1996), suggesting that organizations run a liability risk if they fail to check the criminal backgrounds of their applicants. However, not all ex-offenders repeat past transgressions at the same rate (Kurlychek, Brame, and Bushway, 2006), and not all employers use checks as a definitive means to preclude interviewing and hiring ex-offenders (Pager, 2003). On the contrary, Stoll and Bushway (2008) found that some firms use CBCs to gain additional information about ex-offenders, which sometimes results in higher levels of hiring among ex-offenders than other firms. These results seem to be associated more with firms that are not legally required to perform checks.

Criminal Background Check Process and Higher Education

CBCs have been used in higher education primarily on employees with a "security-sensitive" designation or those who work with minors, with the elderly, and in the medical profession. The "security-sensitive" designation typically applies to those with access to financial and confidential records such as social security numbers and other types of personal identifiable data. This limited application began to change with the case of a former Penn State University engineering professor, Paul E. Krueger, whose criminal background became public when he applied for a state-sanctioned committee. It was discovered through a CBC that the professor had been convicted of three murders in 1965. He had been teaching for fifteen years, four of those at Penn State, before this information became public. This case was followed by the controversy and fear over the possibility that other university employees might have criminal histories including murder, rape, or child molestation.

The public fallout of these cases led to a total of eight states enacting CBC requirements for employees and some student employees at publicly-funded universities. In addition, after the tragic events at both Virginia Tech and Northern Illinois in 2007 and 2008, Maine, Missouri, Virginia and Illinois, mandated that more mental health records be shared with the Federal National Instant Check system (PR Newswire, 2007). In addition, many universities began to develop their own internal policies to address the concerns raised by many of the aforementioned high-profile criminal cases. While these efforts have contributed to more universities utilizing background checks, there are still a surprising number of institutions that still do no background checks at all and an even greater number that do not conduct comprehensive checks across all employees. Hughes and White (2006) evaluated the use of background checks in higher education and found that among 109 administrators, 82 percent (90) conducted CBCs on employees. Within that 82 percent, CBCs were conducted on staff three times more frequently than faculty (74 percent versus 36 percent). The most glaring finding of this research, however, was that a full 18 percent of educational institutions surveyed did not conduct CBCs on any faculty, staff, or students.

While support for the utilization of CBCs has increased across the country, there has been major resistance to these policies from inside universities. Historically, the main resistance to the imposition of background checks has come from the American Association of University Professors (AAUP) who advocated in a 2004 report entitled "Verification and Trust: Background Investigations Preceding Faculty Appointments" that background checks are only necessary for those with "significant security considerations" (AAUP, 2004). The report states that only the need to verify an applicant's qualifications to carry out responsibilities of a specific job justifies an employer's right to compromise the individual's privacy. The report's authors maintain that the background check process is inherently flawed because it relies mainly on a process that has a high probability of delivering inaccurate criminal records and that limits the use of context to properly evaluate the records it does find through this process (Hughes, Hertz, and White, 2009). Additionally, the report's authors suggest that searching the criminal records of faculty members to be an effort of excess relative to the institution's security needs and would represent an unnecessary intrusion of the privacy rights of all faculty.

NEW DIRECTIONS FOR INSTITUTIONAL RESEARCH • DOI: 10.1002/ir

The AAUP's public position on this issue has led many universities to adopt a background check policy that covers only a limited segment of the employee population or specific "security-sensitive" positions as previously outlined. Furthermore, even if universities do move forward with comprehensive background check policies, there are additional legal considerations that must be thought through and addressed.

Legal Issues Associated With Background Checks

It is a reasonable assumption that all colleges and universities seek to provide a safe and secure campus for their students, faculty, and staff. At the same time, and for less altruistic reasons, they also seek to shield themselves from legal liability—and the resulting loss of resources and reputation—should it be determined later that the institution failed to act reasonably in its efforts to provide a safe campus environment.

Unfortunately, simply conducting CBCs does not completely insulate the institution from these risks, and the process itself is fraught with an entirely different array of risks (Hughes, Hertz, and White, 2009). These risks include potential civil liabilities grounded in such legal theories as *respondeat superior*; negligent hiring and negligent retention; or even violations of federal, state, or local antidiscrimination statutes where claims may be asserted based on the legal theories of disparate treatment or disparate impact. Efforts to improve campus security may also trigger unintentional violations of federal or state privacy laws.

For instance, the legal doctrine of *respondeat superior* may impose civil liability on an employer for harm caused to a third party by an employee "acting within the scope of their employment" (a university employee that negligently causes an automobile accident while conducting university business, for example). As a general rule, an employer is not responsible for harm caused by an employee "acting outside of the scope of their employment." However, an increasing number of cases are being reported where an employer has been found liable for harm caused by employees acting outside the scope of their employment. This is especially true where the employer knew or should have known of the employee's propensity to cause undue risk of harm to others (Feliu and Johnson, 2002). Thus, under the legal theories of negligent hiring and negligent retention, civil liability might be imposed on an employer because of its failure to conduct a CBC and uncover such propensities or by retaining an employee whose CBC reveals such propensities.

Claims of discrimination brought under Title VII of the 1964 Civil Rights Act (42 U.S.C., Section 2000e, et seq.) or a myriad of similar state (or in some circumstances local) discrimination statutes also pose risks to colleges and universities seeking to perform CBCs on foreign nationals—who enjoy the protection of these statutes despite their noncitizen status. Potential claims arising from acts of intentional discrimination (disparate treatment) or even unintentional discrimination (disparate impact) as they relate to the implementation of a criminal background check process need to be thoroughly considered and properly addressed.

Finally, privacy laws such as the federal Family Educational Rights and Privacy Act (FERPA) 20 U.S.C. 1232, et seq., 34 CFR Part 99 (and its state equivalent) also have an impact on the use of CBCs in terms of how a CBC is initiated, evaluated, stored, and safeguarded.

Even in states that require CBCs on state universities' faculty, student employees, and staff, the use of international background checks is almost nonexistent. And the same could be said for the higher education community at large. This is primarily due to several factors, including a lack of knowledge about the process itself, insufficient vendor expertise, an assumption that the federal government is already doing CBCs on foreign nationals, and the costs associated with these checks, which often exceed several hundred dollars per applicant.

Homeland Security Initiatives and Universities

In response to the terrorist attacks of September 11, 2001, Congress passed the Public Health Security and Bioterrorism Preparedness and Response Act of 2002 (Preparedness and Response Act) and the Patriot Act. Both pieces of legislation were intended to address some gaps in the security infrastructure of the United States, and both have significant implications for higher education institutions. For example, while the Preparedness and Response Act is intended to improve the ability of the United States to prevent, prepare for, and respond to bioterrorism and other public health emergencies, it has three specific provisions applicable to higher education institutions. Under this law, all colleges and universities that possess select biological agents need to register with the secretary of the U.S. Department of Health and Human Services. The law also requires immediate notification if a select agent has been released inadvertently, lost, or stolen. Therefore, universities need to maintain extensive and detailed inventory lists of select agents. Finally, universities are required to submit the names and other identifying information for individuals whom they determine have a legitimate need to handle or use the biological agents or toxins. The federal government then conducts security assessments of these individuals to determine if any of them are on what is known as a restricted status list. The security assessment will use any available criminal, immigration, national security, and other electronic databases that are available to the federal government to conduct background checks on the registered individuals. The university must then deny access to the agents or toxins by those who are deemed to be "restricted persons" by virtue of their presence in any of these databases.

NEW DIRECTIONS FOR INSTITUTIONAL RESEARCH • DOI: 10.1002/ir

The Patriot Act, designed to intercept and obstruct terrorist activities, also has a number of provisions with a direct impact on higher education including provisions surrounding FERPA, the Electronics Communication Privacy Act (ECPA), the Foreign Intelligence Surveillance Act (FISA), and SEVIS. In the case of FERPA, the Patriot Act amends FERPA by creating a procedure through which the U.S. Department of Justice may seek a court order to collect educational records deemed relevant to an investigation or prosecution of terrorism as an exception to the standard requirements for confidentiality of student records.

The Patriot Act also amended provisions of ECPA, which was intended to strengthen the privacy surrounding electronic communications, including provisions for securing warrants to conduct wiretaps or accessing voice mail data. The act amended these protections and now allows federal authorities easier access to securing these warrants. In the case of FISA, originally adopted in 1978, investigations of criminal activity suspected of having been backed by a "hostile foreign power" are partially exempt from the Fourth Amendment's proscriptions against warrantless searches and seizures. Post Patriot Act, FISA expands the possible categories under which the law would apply and also broadens the number of individuals who could be covered by the law, including librarians and Internet service providers. The law also limits what can be disclosed about these investigations by those forced to comply. Finally, the Patriot Act had an impact on the pace of implementation surrounding the Student Exchange Visitor Information System (SEVIS). SEVIS is a web-based system intended to track foreign students and scholars once they arrive in the United States to begin their studies. The system was enacted in 1996, but implementation lagged for a number of reasons. The passage of the Patriot Act required compliance by universities by the start of the 2003–2004 academic year or face significant financial penalties. The system is intended to establish an electronic system to collect data on foreign students enrolled in American colleges and universities for their duration of study and exchange visitors in the country for short stays.

Student Visa Process and CBC Processes

Citizens of other countries who wish to visit the United States for the purpose of study, cultural exchanges, business, or tourism generally must apply for a nonimmigrant visa at a U.S. embassy or consulate. Those who wish to apply to study in the United States may apply for any of the various student visas including F visas (for academic study at a two- or four-year institution), M visas (for vocational study), and J visas (for cultural exchange programs). H-1B visas are for foreign nationals with at least a bachelor's degree who are needed for specialty positions in the United States. These visas are typically limited to approximately eighty-five thousand annually. In general, though, academic workers recruited for employment at U.S. universities are not subject to these limits. F visas are the most common type of student visa issued to foreign nationals and are typically for the duration of study. The most important distinctions among the various student visa types are the requirements dealing with employment status once the student arrives in the United States. For all F and J visa holders, students are allowed to work on campus but not outside the campus environment, except in the case of practical training programs required as part of the degree program (Canter and Siegel, 2007).

A multistep process, with documentation reviews, personal interviews, fingerprinting, and cross-referencing of the applicant into the Consular Lookout and Support System (CLASS), is used for determining who will be issued a student visa. CLASS references records provided by various agencies, including information on immigration violations, visa refusals, and terrorism concerns (Ford, 2005). The process begins when the visa applicant makes an appointment at the embassy or consulate in his or her area. The applicant arrives with required documentation, including the visa application, personal documents verifying identity, financial records verifying the applicant has the financial means for self-support while in the academic program, and the I-20 form, which a college or university sends to a foreign student who has been accepted into a school's academic program. This form contains all relevant information regarding the applicant's term of study, field of study, level of study (undergraduate or graduate), expected beginning and completion dates, and the applicant's ability to pay for his or her education.

The applicant's visa application will ask the applicant to self-disclose any set of circumstances that might make him or her inadmissible for a visa approval, including links with terrorists, criminal backgrounds, likelihood of needing financial assistance once in the United States, and certain physical or mental disabilities. The individual's material is then run through the CLASS system and assuming there is no "hit" in the system, the consular officer determines whether to grant the visa or not. In the event that a "hit" is discovered in the CLASS system, the applicant must submit a set of fingerprints to be checked against those in the FBI's NCIC's Interstate Identification Index to verify the authenticity of the "hit" and then the applicant is either approved for a visa or not. Finally, if the visa applicant's background or proposed activity in the United States will involve working with or exposure to technologies on the federal government's Technology Alert List, then the consular officer will request a Visa Mantis check. The State Department's Bureau of Nonproliferation, the FBI, and other agencies will review the information provided in the Visa Mantis request, conduct an investigation, and then issue a ruling to direct whether the visa application should be approved (Ford, 2005).

Once a student is approved for a visa, he or she must make arrangements to travel to the United States within thirty days of the start of the school's academic program. There is no flexibility to arrive more than thirty days before the start of the academic program on a student visa. A student who wants to arrive later than thirty days must also apply for and qualify for a visitor visa to cover the additional time he or she will be in the United States prior to the start of the academic cycle.

Once the student arrives in the United States, Customs and Border Protection (CBP) officials will process the student through customs. Upon the completion of the interview process, CBP officials do have the authority to deny entry to the students even though they already cleared the Department of State's (DOS) screening process in their home country of origin. CBP's actions are intended to provide one additional layer to the anti-terrorism efforts embedded throughout the visa process. If the student is approved for entry, the applicant's arrival is reported to Immigration and Custom Enforcement (ICE), where information is loaded into SEVIS. Thereafter, the university has the responsibility to input applicant information into the SEVIS database based on any change in the student's enrollment status (which must be done within twenty-one days of the change) or living situation (which must be done within ten days of changes).

Despite the increasing shift toward more use of CBCs on domestic employees and students, little, if any, emphasis has been given to implementing these checks on foreign employees or students. This lack of emphasis is due to the fact that most university administrators have long believed that the visa application process provides the requisite background checks needed to cover issues of criminal behavior. As identified in the previous section, there are limited efforts to conduct more thorough background checks on individuals applying for nonimmigrant visas unless this individual has self-reported a reason to initiate the check or the applicant has registered a "hit" in the government's anti-terrorism databases search.

Prior to 2002, immigration and oversight of the visa process was the sole responsibility of the State Department following passage of the 1952 Immigration and Nationality Act. A shared responsibility emerged after the terrorist events of September 11, 2001, when it was discovered that seventeen of the nineteen terrorists associated with the 9/11 events had entered the United States on a variety of temporary or student visas. These events led to the adoption of the Homeland Security Act of 2002, which was intended to strengthen the visa process without limiting legitimate travel by foreign nationals. The fact that foreign students who come to the United States for study are estimated to contribute approximately $14.5 billion to the economy underscores the need to create an effective balance between strengthening security and facilitating legitimate travel (McCormack, Neelakantan, and Overland, 2007).

Although the act did not take the visa process away from the State Department, it did provide for the assignment of Department of Homeland

Security (DHS) employees to U.S. embassies and consulates to provide expert advice and visa security training to state department consular officers (Ford, 2005). The program was initially intended to target consular posts in Saudi Arabia and mandated the review of all visa applications originating within Saudi Arabia. Ultimately the intent of the act has been to expand the presence of DHS visa security officers (VSOs) to other consulates and embassies deemed high risk by the U.S. government. A 2005 Government Accountability Office (GAO) report suggested there were significant problems with the implementation of this program, affecting the probability of rolling out the program to embassies and consulates outside Saudi Arabia (Ford, 2005).

Implications

As discussed above, the previous process to apply for a student visa highlighted some significant gaps in the security clearance protocol. These gaps were reinforced when, in 2007, two University of South Florida students, Ahmed Mohamed and Yousseh Megahed, were charged with terrorism-related crimes after police found pipe bombs in the back of their vehicle following a routine traffic stop. According to federal records, Mohamed had previously been arrested on terrorism charges in his native Egypt for producing a video on building a remote-controlled car bomb. Both students had entered the United States through the visa process and were enrolled as full-time students. At the time of his arrest, Mohamed was actually employed as a graduate student in the university's engineering department (VanSickle and Jenkins, 2007). It was also subsequently discovered that he had two different passports in his apartment issued under two different names. In June 2008, Mohamed pled guilty to providing material support to terrorists (Ryan, 2008).

This information suggests that our existing process for conducting security checks in overseas consulates is still quite flawed. The prior circumstances revealed that the nonimmigrant student visa process allowed individuals into the United States under seemingly fraudulent conditions. The situations strongly indicate a need for an overhaul of the visa process. Furthermore, given the ability of both J and F visa holders to work in on-campus settings (and off-campus training programs for F visa holders), the reliance of universities on the due diligence process of the federal government may actually expose the university to additional liability if one of these visa holders, with a prior criminal record, engages in criminal activity while in the employment of the university. Since it is likely that most F, J, H-1B, and M visa holders will not have gone through a criminal background check, universities may face assumed responsibility if they decide to hire these students and therefore expose their institutions to potential liability for the criminal behavior of their student employees.

Conclusion

While the trend toward the use of CBCs on domestic employees and even students has increased on most college campuses, the use of CBCs on foreign employees and students has been virtually nonexistent even as overall foreign enrollment increases. Laws enacted since the terrorist attacks of 2001 may have been intended and are assumed to have reduced some of the risk of bringing foreign applicants with a criminal past to campus; however, the evidence presented in this chapter counters that assumption. Some strengthening is apparent, but the reliance on self-reporting or prior recorded acts of terrorism as the means of identifying an employee or student posing a threat to safety and security remains clearly insufficient. The acceptance of CBCs in the hiring process of public and private sector entities has grown with these trends. However, the application of this process is far from universal or consistent. Reliance on the process is even less common relative to foreign individuals working or studying in U.S. colleges and businesses.

In the years since 9/11, steps have been taken to make workplaces and campuses safer. The inadequacies in the enacted legislation, however, create a threat that must be mitigated or removed if employers in higher education are to manage their exposure to liability and provide safe and secure work environments.

References

American Association of University Professors (AAUP). "Verification and Trust: Background Investigations Preceding Faculty Appointments." Washington, D.C.: American Association of University Professors, 2004.

Canter, L. A., and Siegel, M. S. *U.S. Immigration Made Easy.* Berkeley, Calif.: Nolo, 2007.

Catholic University. "Summary of Federal Laws." 2008. Retrieved Mar. 29, 2009, from http://74.125.47.132/search?q=cache:Ta2R4bhUHxAJ:counsel.cua.edu/fedlaw/bpra .cfm+ percent22Bioterrorism+Preparedness+and+Response+Act+of+2002 percent22 +and+ percent22higher+education percent22&cd=2&hl=en&ct=clnk&gl=us.

Connerly, M. L., Arvey, R. D., and Bernardy, C. J. "Criminal Background Checks for Prospective and Current Employees: Current Practices Among Municipal Agencies." *Public Personnel Management,* 2001, *30*(2), 173–183.

Feliu, A. G., and Johnson, W. T., Jr. *Negligence in Employment Law.* Washington, D.C.: BNA Books, 2002.

Ford, J. *Border Security: Actions Needed to Strengthen Management of Department of Homeland Security's Visa Security Program.* Washington, D.C.: U.S. Government Accountability Office, 2005.

Gardner, S. "Does Your Background Checker Put You in Jeopardy? A Case for Best Practices and Due Diligence." *Journal of Ethical, Legal and Regulatory Issues, 11*(2), July 2008. Retrieved May 17, 2010, from http://findarticles.com/p/articles/mi_ m1TOS/is_2_11/ai_n31140815/?tag=content;col1.

Gendreau, P., Little, T., and Goggin, C. "A Meta-Analysis of Predictors of Adult Offender Recidivism." *Criminology,* 1996, 34, 401–433.

NEW DIRECTIONS FOR INSTITUTIONAL RESEARCH • DOI: 10.1002/ir

Hughes, S. F., Hertz, G., and White, R. J. "Criminal Background Checks in U.S. Higher Education: A Review of Policy Developments, Process Implementations and Post-Results Evaluation Procedures." Unpublished manuscript, 2009.

Hughes, S. F., and White, R. J. "Risk Mitigation in Higher Education: An Overview of the Use of Background Checks on Campus." *CUPA-HR Journal*, 2006, 57(2), 23–32.

Kurlycheck, M., Brame, R., and Bushway, S. D. "Scarlet Letters and Recidivism: Does Old Criminal Record Predict Future Offending?" *Criminology and Public Policy*, 2006, 5, 483–504.

Langan, P. A., and Levine, D. J. *Recidivism of Prisoners Released in 1994*. Washington, D.C.: U.S. Department of Justice, Bureau of Justice Statistics, 2002.

Maslen, G. "US: Record Number of Foreign Students." *University World News*, 2008. Retrieved Feb. 28, 2009, from http://www.universityworldnews.com/article.php?story=20081120154841183.

McCormack, E., Neelakantan, S., and Overland, M. A. "Number of Foreign Students Bounces Back to Near-Record High." *Chronicle of Higher Education*, Nov. 16, 2007, 54(12), A1–A36.

Pager, D. "The Mark of a Criminal Record." *American Journal of Sociology*, 2003, 108, 937–975.

PR Newswire. "Four States Have Now Taken Steps to Strengthen Background Checks in Aftermath of Virginia Tech." Dateline: Washington, July 6, 2007.

Ryan, J. "Egyptian Student in U.S. Pleads Guilty in Fla. Terrorism Case." 2008. Retrieved Mar. 21, 2009, from http://abcnews.go.com/TheLaw/story?id=5193198&page=.

Stoll, M. A., and Bushway, S. D. "The Effect of Criminal Background Checks on Hiring Ex-Offenders." *Criminology and Public Policy*, 2008, 7(3), 371–404.

U.S. Department of Justice Statistics. "Correctional Populations." 2007. Retrieved Mar. 21, 2009, from http://www.ojp.usdoj.gov/bjs/glance/tables/corr2tab.htm.

VanSickle, A., and Jenkins, C. "Car's Explosive Contents Revealed at Hearing for USF Students." 2007. Retrieved Mar. 21, 2009, from http://blogs.tampabay.com/breakingnews/2007/09/usf-student-won.html.

STEPHANIE HUGHES *is an assistant professor of management at Northern Kentucky University.*

EILEEN WEISENBACH KELLER *is an assistant professor of marketing at Northern Kentucky University.*

GILES T. HERTZ *is an assistant professor of management at Northern Kentucky University.*

NEW DIRECTIONS FOR INSTITUTIONAL RESEARCH • DOI: 10.1002/ir

5

The SEVIS program, one component of the federal guidelines for homeland security, continues to affect higher education institutions.

SEVIS: The Impact of Homeland Security on American Colleges and Universities

Janet V. Danley

In the days following the horrific events of September 11, 2001, many in the international educators' community wondered what the future would bring. Allegations that international students, or at least people who pretended to be international students, were involved in the tragic acts were widely reported in the media. There was a steady drumbeat of demand from the Bush administration and the public for better control, monitoring, and enforcement of visa regulations on international students and scholars.

Indeed, as investigations of those who perpetrated these acts of aggression continued, alarm spread over what appeared to be lax monitoring of international students' and scholars' movements and activities. Staff and faculty responsible for recruiting, admitting, and enrolling international students were aware that beginning as early as the mid-1990s, the Immigration and Naturalization Service (INS) was considering initiatives to develop a management system for international students and scholars. These initiatives, such as the Illegal Immigration Reform and Immigrant Responsibility Act of 1996 (IIRIRA), which resulted in the Coordinated Interagency Partnership Regulating International Students (CIPRIS) system, were to provide international educators and their institutions tools to monitor international students and scholars more closely. In the days following 9/11, revelations of lost and missing international students accumulated. International educators and administrators expected stringent

NEW DIRECTIONS FOR INSTITUTIONAL RESEARCH, no. 146, Summer 2010 © Wiley Periodicals, Inc.
Published online in Wiley InterScience (www.interscience.wiley.com) • DOI: 10.1002/ir.343

protocols for monitoring and enforcing visa regulations on international students would be the undoubted outcome. Within a month of 9/11, the Student and Exchange Visitor Information System (SEVIS) came into existence (Rosser, Hermsen, Mamiseishvili, and Wood, 2007; Kurz and Scannell, 2002).

Preimplementation

In the years preceding the national nightmare of 9/11, American higher education enjoyed a high reputation around the world. Any man or woman who earned a degree at an American college or university could be certain of a successful professional career when he or she returned home because of the prestige of U.S. higher education. The United States benefited as well from the contributions international students made in research, technology development, the arts, and athletics while they were students on U.S. campuses. Where once international students found an inviting and welcoming environment on American campuses, the events of September 11, 2001, changed, perhaps forever, the way Americans view international students and how the world perceives the United States (Martin, 2008). The world no longer views American higher education with as much favor because of 9/11 and the way the federal government and the public reacted (Bagnato, 2005; Kurz and Scannell, 2002; Martin, 2008; Wong, 2006).

As sensitive as most educators were to the unimaginable horrors that 9/11 visited on the American public, the introduction of SEVIS took the international educators' community by surprise. SEVIS was a major component of the Uniting and Strengthening America by Providing Appropriate Tools Required to Intercept and Obstruct Terrorism Act (USA PATRIOT Act), which was quickly enacted by Congress. Many educators believed the provisions of the Patriot Act overreacted to events of September 11, 2001, and the January 30, 2003, SEVIS implementation deadline was criticized as unrealistic and a near-impossible expectation (Kurz and Scannell, 2002; Wong, 2006). Furthermore, the complexities of SEVIS, an unfunded federal mandate, created serious concerns at colleges and universities. Professional educational associations such as NAFSA, the Association of International Educators, the American Council on Education (ACE), the American Association of Collegiate Registrars and Admissions Officers (AACRAO), and the National Association of State Universities and Land-Grant Colleges (NASULGC), among others, had objections to SEVIS. At every opportunity, American institutions and organizations expressed their objections to many of the law's provisions (Wong, 2006).

Among the most criticized provisions of the law were the fees assessed on international students, which the law initially would have required colleges and universities to collect and remit to the federal government. Vociferous complaint over the fee collection proviso of the law caused lawmakers and regulators to relent. A rewriting of the fee collection provision shifted the responsibility for fee collection to the embassies and consulates issuing the visas.

The twenty-one-day reporting requirement also caused concern at institutions. This requirement mandated that nearly any change in the student's status be reported within twenty-one days of occurrence, a departure from practices in the registrar's office that captured data changes during course registration. The change to a twenty-one-day reporting window required reengineering many business processes in the registrar's and international programs offices.

Perhaps the most onerous aspect of SEVIS was the associated cost of implementation and maintenance of systems that colleges and universities now needed to comply with the law. Some schools approached the systems issue by contracting with one of the third-party software developers that had created interface applications for batched data submissions into the SEVIS databases. Other schools imposed the task of developing the SEVIS interface application on their information technology departments. Yet other schools depended on their integrated systems vendors (Datatel, PeopleSoft, ACT, and others) to deliver appropriate modules or patches to interface with SEVIS. However, all of these interface application solutions carried hefty price tags that campuses would have to absorb (Kurz and Scannell, 2002).

Personnel needs created another considerable cost for a number of colleges and universities. Many schools quickly recognized that SEVIS would have a significant impact on staff workload, not only in the international students and scholars offices, but also throughout the enrollment services functions of the institution. A number of campuses created a new position, with titles such as SEVIS Coordinator or SEVIS Director. The individuals hired for the position managed everything from staff, faculty, and student training to the technical aspects of the SEVIS implementation (Kurz and Scannell, 2002; Rosser, Hermsen, Mamiseishvili, and Wood, 2007).

Institutions with moderate to large international student and scholar populations, such as Washington State University, seemed particularly vulnerable to these costs and the tight time frame of the implementation (Danley, 2002; Wong, 2006). In fall 2002, Washington State University enrolled 22,166 students, 1,255 of whom were international students. In addition, the university employed approximately 150 international scholars (Danley, 2002). Other colleges and universities with much larger international student and scholar populations reeled under the implications of such a significant undertaking as SEVIS represented (Wong, 2006).

Recognizing that SEVIS would necessitate a reexamination of the business processes for international student admissions and records maintenance for continuing international students, the international programs and the enrollment services staff at WSU initiated a series of discussions with students, faculty, staff, and administrators at the university. These discussions forced the university community to take a focused look at the role of international education and international students at the institution. In addition to developing plans to redesign business practices in order to comply with SEVIS, a renewed appreciation for international education evolved. The WSU faculty and administration had always placed a high value on the contributions international students made to research, athletics, and the university's diversity. Following the faculty and administration's long look at international education, the WSU community resolved to protect the university's ability to attract and admit international students while ensuring students' rights during the SEVIS implementation (Danley, 2002).

The ongoing discussions with WSU staff also focused on what student data would be required for SEVIS compliance. As the implementation deadline approached and because the SEVIS regulations and the SEVIS database were developing at an agonizingly slow pace, many more questions arose than initially could be answered by the federal regulators, leaving WSU and other campuses in limbo. The staff in the WSU international programs and admissions offices felt forced to make best-guess decisions on the data elements that would be required for the SEVIS database record for each student. At WSU, international students submitted the majority of the data needed for the SEVIS database on the admission application, but some key data items that staff anticipated would be required for SEVIS were missing. The WSU enrollment services and admissions staff worked together to modify the application materials for international undergraduate and graduate students to include all of the required data anticipated for SEVIS compliance. During the same period, the international programs staff discovered that a number of campus offices collected data from international students for a variety of purposes. However, the design of the university's main student record database did not accept these additional data. The answer to all of these data quandaries was a centralized data warehouse. WSU therefore purchased a third-party software package to centralize, organize, and manage all of the data collected on campus needed for SEVIS databases (Danley, 2002).

Concurrent with the discussions about data collection, WSU staff reviewed the work flows and duty assignments in the offices responsible for data collection. In the proposed law, access to the SEVIS system was limited to the primary designated school official (PDSO), the designated school officials (DSO), and the administrative school officials (ADSO). The limited access would affect how employees completed the necessary administrative and clerical work for SEVIS data input. Employee work flows required procedural reengineering to ensure compliance with SEVIS data submission requirements.

Throughout late spring and early summer 2002, focus continued on developing work flow and duty assignments for WSU staff. Administrative oversight for the SEVIS implementation was a consideration since the international programs, admissions, and registrar's offices had few spare personnel or time to deploy the SEVIS program to meet the upcoming implementation deadline. In answer to the workload dilemma, WSU hired a SEVIS coordinator and assigned him the responsibility for initial deployment and staff training.

The SEVIS coordinator and the international programs staff, understanding that international students could possibly be confused and caught off guard by the regulations that were going to be more rigorously enforced, developed a detailed SEVIS training program for both students and campus staff. Although the student requirements did not change significantly with the SEVIS implementation, the reporting requirements were very different from previous INS regulations. Under SEVIS, the consequences of failing to report student status or demographic changes to INS (DHS) could be dire for the students and the university. In an effort to prepare students, the SEVIS coordinator and the international programs staff worked tirelessly during the final months of fall semester 2002 to inform the students of the changes imposed by the SEVIS implementation. University staff members worked collaboratively throughout the remainder of the fall 2002 and into early January 2003 to finalize the SEVIS implementation at Washington State University.

Postimplementation

Since 2002, colleges and universities across the nation have implemented SEVIS and are using either third-party developed applications or the federal interface for data reporting (Wong, 2006). I followed the experiences of several colleges and universities in Idaho and Washington State as the institutions completed the initial deployment and subsequent compliance with SEVIS and the Department of Homeland Security (DHS) regulation of the international student and scholar monitoring system. Since the SEVIS deployment, colleges and universities have coped with the new rules and regulations and the significant staffing and budgetary consequences with mixed success (Wong, 2006).

Impact of Implementation. In the post-9/11 era, there have been changes to the legal and policy landscape surrounding international student education. The vocabulary has changed, agency names have changed, and responsibilities and organizations have shifted during the interval since implementation.

International students wanting to study in the United States continue to face innumerable hurdles in the SEVIS postimplementation era (Martin, 2008). Colleges, universities, and even lawmakers recognize that although the number of applications for student visas is increasing after steep declines during the six years following 9/11, U.S. higher education lost momentum in attracting international students and scholars due in large part to the difficulties they face in obtaining and maintaining educational visas (Bagnato, 2005; Maslen, 2008). The lack of communication and contradictory information emanating from DHS and the Department of State (DOS) with regard to changing SEVIS requirements and restrictions, especially when the changes affect students' status, has continued to frustrate international educators and other staff at many campuses (Bagnato, 2005).

Aside from the difficulties for students and scholars, staff charged with maintaining SEVIS also face challenges. The workloads of the professionals who work with international students and scholars or the SEVIS system not only dramatically increased but also became unmanageable. As a result, colleges and universities lost and are continuing to lose key employees to burnout and frustration (Rosser, Hermsen, Mamiseishvili, and Wood, 2007). Budget reductions caused by the economic downturn are creating hardships for institutions trying to attract and hire qualified professionals to replace these employees.

One of the most significant difficulties reported by staff responsible for inputting and maintaining student data face is their perception that there is a zero tolerance for mistakes made in the SEVIS system (Rosser, Hermsen, Mamiseishvili, and Wood, 2007). If a mistake occurs, the school's staff cannot correct the mistake but instead must contact the SEVIS Service Center to request a data correction (Bagnato, 2005; Wong, 2006). DHS makes no exceptions or allowances to the data correction procedures, citing the need to protect data integrity and safeguard the system, even when the mistake is a result of a system error or glitch (Wong, 2006; Rosser, Hermsen, Mamiseishvili, and Wood, 2007). In some cases, delays in correcting errors have resulted in students' falling out of status (Bagnato, 2005; Wong, 2006).

Some institutions report that the admissions process for international students has improved and become more consistent because the SEVIS requirements for data collection standardize the process. Other schools describe greater complexity and increased bureaucracy as an outcome of the SEVIS regulation (Rosser, Hermsen, Mamiseishvili, and Wood, 2007). The following sections present descriptions of four schools' experiences in the SEVIS postimplementation period drawn from my interviews with staff.

Washington State University. Robert Rigg, SEVIS coordinator at Washington State University (WSU), reports that the university weathered the pre- and postimplementation phases of the SEVIS system successfully. Rigg observes that WSU has successfully integrated the SEVIS data requirements into the institution's business processes in all of the departments responsible for SEVIS compliance. "Although the main responsibility [for SEVIS compliance] is with the office of international student and scholars, undergraduate admissions, the graduate school, the Intensive

American Language Center, and the three branch campus locations all have designated school officials (DSOs) now and these individuals assist with parts of the SEVIS processes," says Rigg. He also reports good support from the executive administration for the procedural and budgetary needs that arise to remain in compliance with SEVIS regulation and requirement (Robert Rigg, personal communication, Mar. 2009).

In addition to creating DSO positions, the university established a SEVIS coordinator position early in the process. The coordinator is responsible for the time-consuming work of ensuring that data reporting is accurate and timely, among many other responsibilities. Rigg states that WSU's recognition of the need for this key position in part explains the ease of implementation WSU experienced.

Although there continue to be maintenance fees and expenses, Rigg reports that the significant initial budget outlays to install SEVIS interface software and the initial changes to business practices are now fully absorbed. Rigg states that the budgetary impacts that once were cause for concern are no longer significant. The largest expenditure that the SEVIS system requires is staff time. Rigg states that with more experience and training, staff time dedicated to SEVIS has declined somewhat, although regular changes to SEVIS reporting requirements and regulations challenge the staff.

With respect to WSU's international student and scholar community, Rigg notes that the students and scholars are now well aware of their responsibilities for maintaining frequent contact with the international students and scholar office in order to protect their status. Rigg believes the intensive orientation students and scholars receive on arrival helps new students and scholars understand the requirements. There was only a minimal impact on WSU's ability to recruit and enroll international students, according to Rigg.

Rigg concludes that SEVIS changed the people-oriented culture of the international students and scholars office to a more technical, data-oriented culture.

University of Idaho. Tammi Johnson, coordinator of international student, scholar, and faculty services in the international programs office, states that the university has adapted, with many staffing changes, to SEVIS. Johnson says, "SEVIS has required additional staffing as well as additional training. We also had to add campuses to our I-17 [the petition form submitted by the institution to gain access to the SEVIS system and authority to admit and enroll international students and to hire international scholars], and we are now required to have DSOs at each of those campuses. We also had to purchase VisaManager [a third-party software application] for batch processing." The international programs office is the primary unit responsible for SEVIS, according to Johnson. She adds that each campus has a DSO staff position, which may be located in other offices besides international programs (Tammi Johnson, personal communication, Mar. 2009).

Johnson reports that the financial impact on the university has been significant, although she notes that SEVIS takes budget priority simply because failing to budget for SEVIS adequately would adversely affect the university's ability to recruit and enroll international students. The purchase of VisaManager, in addition to the extra staffing needs, requires a significant allocation from the overall international programs budget, according to Johnson.

Student recruiting and enrollments are beginning to improve after tumbling to record lows following 9/11, reports Johnson. She states that the students and scholars are aware of the SEVIS requirements to maintain status. However, she notes that the international programs office sends frequent and repeated reminders and updates about every two weeks to the students and she believes this helps keep students on top of their responsibilities.

In Johnson's opinion, although SEVIS was supposed to take the staff in international student management and monitoring into a paperless era, the record keeping is actually more difficult since SEVIS implementation. In addition to the sheer volume of information that must be collected and maintained for individual students, the constant updates and rules changes to SEVIS make work difficult for offices, particularly those with small staffs, "to keep up with everything," while trying to meet the needs of the students and scholars. As a result, Johnson says that she and her staff feel that their contact with the students is limited.

Lewis-Clark State College. Diane Douglas, director of admissions and registrar at Lewis-Clark State College (LCSC) in Lewiston, Idaho, reports that SEVIS caused this small four-year school to completely overhaul the way staff deal with international students. Douglas goes on to say that SEVIS changed the role of the international student services office (now known as international programs office) from a student support role to that of enforcer. Overall, however, LCSC successfully survived the SEVIS implementation, according to Douglas. She further notes that there is now a straightforward chain of command within the international programs office. The International Programs office staff and faculty follow detailed processes for notification and problem solving for issues that arise (Diane Douglas, personal communication, Feb. 2009).

Douglas reports that ongoing costs of licensing, training, and maintenance for SEVIS limit the college's ability to recruit international students aggressively because less money is available than in the past. Recent budget cuts mandated by the Idaho state legislature are creating unanticipated challenges for the international students and staff. To address the budget reductions, there are fewer scheduled courses, and some academic programs have been dropped. Consequently international students are facing difficulties maintaining their required full-time enrollment status.

NEW DIRECTIONS FOR INSTITUTIONAL RESEARCH • DOI: 10.1002/ir

The challenges for the staff to stay abreast of changes to the SEVIS rules and data requirements are taxing for a small school, Douglas says. She notes that the international programs office employees try to take as much burden off other offices as possible. However, the clerical time required to input all of the students' data manually into SEVIS is overwhelming for the small international programs staff, so some of the workload migrated to other offices such as admissions and the registrar's office, according to Douglas.

The international students, for the most part, are complying with SEVIS status requirements, according to Douglas. However, she notes that students from some regions, particularly Asia and Africa, harbor great fear of falling out of status and exhibit significant stress that the reporting of their data is correct and on time. Other students may not recognize the need to maintain continuous communication with the SEVIS coordinator.

Complying with SEVIS, Douglas concludes, has resulted in some unexpected twists and turns for the college. Prior to SEVIS, LCSC had little to do with agencies such as the border patrol, the DHS (and INS prior to DHS), the Federal Bureau of Investigation (FBI), and other agencies. In addition, international programs employees are discovering that less affluent international students need more help coping with financial worries, particularly related to their status. Douglas is concerned that students will be tempted to work illegally, imperiling their status.

Walla Walla Community College. Sandra Leonetti, in the office of admissions and records at Walla Walla Community College (WWCC) of Washington State, says that the college has successfully mastered the SEVIS requirements. She reports that the admissions process and preparing I-20s for the students "has become much smoother and easier since the implementation of SEVIS." She further notes that transferring students in from other institutions is much easier than in the past. Leonetti believes it is also easier to keep track of the changes to U.S. admission procedures through SEVIS with the nearly continuous stream of e-mail alerts, unlike the previous means that INS used to inform colleges and universities through letters mailed to the president of the college (Sandra Leonetti, personal communication, Mar. 2009).

In counterpoint to the staffing challenges other institutions have suffered, WWCC has not experienced staffing changes because of SEVIS. Leonetti notes that staff work together to submit data for international students' records through the manual data inputting screens. The employees in the office of admissions and records are primarily responsible for all SEVIS data submission and maintenance.

The budget impact from the SEVIS implementation has been negligible in Leonetti's opinion, "probably because the college's international student population was not large enough to warrant purchasing additional software to handle SEVIS." The only continuing direct cost, according to Leonetti, is the annual relicensing fee, which is budgeted each year.

Leonetti states that the international students at WWCC appear to understand and comply with the SEVIS requirements without complaint. She notes that WWCC faculty and staff help new international students understand the rules.

In summary, Leonetti considers WWCC's transition to SEVIS relatively free of the problems and issues that have caused some other colleges and universities such difficulties. Leonetti, in fact, believes that serving international students is easier than in pre-SEVIS days.

Conclusion

From a review of the literature and in interviews with staff at four colleges and universities, each institution's experience and transition to SEVIS compliance appears unique. For some schools, compliance with SEVIS rules is a lengthy, time-consuming, and costly endeavor. For others, the process appears straightforward. While officials within and close to the Bush administration judged SEVIS to be a total success, educators and administrators at many colleges and universities are not convinced (Bagnato, 2005; Wong, 2006).

From a practical standpoint, SEVIS continues to frustrate college employees responsible for complying with the myriad array of rules and regulations. Nearly continuous change plagues the system and challenges the individuals who must make the system work. Ongoing costs from relicensing and maintenance are challenging budget administrators' ability to balance the books. The expectations and requirements to remain in good SEVIS status stymie and confuse students at times.

With reference to policy, SEVIS accomplished centralization of the control and monitoring of international students and scholars. However, many believe that security concerns took precedence over and eroded the status and leadership of U.S. higher education around the world. There appeared to be a complete and total disregard of institutions' educational philosophies in the development and deployment of SEVIS. Finally, in the haste to force SEVIS onto the higher education landscape, the policy and rules makers often ignored the educational needs and goals of the students coming to the United States for their college education. Rather than a welcoming and inviting environment, too many prospective international students discover an overzealous, unfriendly, and intolerant atmosphere. Consequently, for many years, fewer international students were interested in attending American colleges and universities and chose other countries for their college study. Indeed, it has only been in recent years that American colleges and universities have experienced a rebound in the numbers of international students applying for admission (Bagnato, 2005; Wong, 2006; Maslen, 2008).

References

Bagnato, K. "Obtaining Student Visas Remains an Endurance Test." *Black Issues in Higher Education,* 2005, 22(5), 7.

Danley, J. *SEVIS: One Institution's Tale of Implementation.* 2002. Retrieved Mar. 2, 2009, from http://www.pacrao.org/docs/resources/writersteam/SEVIS.doc.

Kurz, K., and Scannell, J. "Dodging SEVIS Snafus." *University Business,* 2002, 5(10), 13–14.

Martin, N. "Foreign Students View U.S. Education as Superior." 2008. Retrieved Feb. 26, 2009, from http://www.prweb.com/releases/2008/07/prweb1111954.htm.

Maslen, G. "US: Record Number of Foreign Students." *University World News,* 2008. Retrieved Feb. 28, 2009, from http://www.universityworldnews.com/article.php?story=20081120154841183.

Rosser, V., Hermsen, J., Mamiseishvili, K., and Wood, M. "A National Study Examining the Impact of SEVIS on International Student and Scholar Advisors." *Higher Education,* 2007, 54(4), 525–542.

Wong, K. "Implementing the USA PATRIOT Act: A Case Study of the Student and Exchange Visitor Information System (SEVIS)." *Brigham Young University Education and Law Journal,* 2006, 2, 379–454.

JANET V. DANLEY *is the executive director of Walla Walla Community College–Clarkston Campus.*

NEW DIRECTIONS FOR INSTITUTIONAL RESEARCH • DOI: 10.1002/ir

6

This chapter describes how data derived from geographic information systems (GIS) can be used to reinforce and integrate emergency operation plans at institutions of higher learning.

Uses of GIS for Homeland Security and Emergency Management for Higher Education Institutions

Stuart B. Murchison

Geographic information systems (GIS) are a major component of the geospatial sciences, which are also composed of geostatistical analysis, remote sensing, and global positional satellite systems. These systems can be integrated into GIS for georeferencing, pattern analysis, visualization, and understanding spatial concepts that transcend conventional academic disciplines. There are many elegant definitions of GIS, and the correct uses of it can assist analysts and decision makers in their quest to answer spatial questions and issues (Aitken and Michel, 2007; Chrisman, 1999; Teodorescu, 2003). Cutter (2003) contends that GIS can be classified as "1. spatial data acquisition and integration; 2. distributing computing; 3. dynamic representation of physical and human processes; 4. cognition of geographic information; 5. interoperability; 6. scale, spatial analysis, and uncertainty; 7. decision support systems" (p. 442). The tragedies of September 11, 2001, led many governments, quasi-governmental entities, and private businesses to seriously consider the use of GIS to assess their infrastructure, attempt to identify and protect assets, integrate emergency operation centers with GIS, and use GIS in emergency response systems (Murchison, 2003). Higher educational institutions have lagged behind in their support efforts in using GIS for their homeland security and emergency management needs. Many of the reasons for this lag are discussed in

NEW DIRECTIONS FOR INSTITUTIONAL RESEARCH, no. 146, Summer 2010 © Wiley Periodicals, Inc.
Published online in Wiley InterScience (www.interscience.wiley.com) • DOI: 10.1002/ir.344

this chapter, as well as how initiating policy at higher institutions that do use GIS will assist those that are resisting GIS implementation.

Homeland Security and Emergency Management Threats

Institutions of higher learning have the same potential for disasters as any other public or private entities. These disasters can manifest themselves as natural hazards, technological hazards, and human-induced hazards, and therefore the institution is responsible for reacting, managing, and recovering from any type of harmful situation that might occur (Federal Emergency Management Agency [FEMA], 2004; Johnson, 2003). Of the myriad natural and technological disasters that can threaten educational institutions, many become more obvious because of their spatial orientation, such as latitude, proximity to coastlines, climatic externalities, topographic orientation, population density, and campus aspect; and the levels of technology present, such as computer and networking expertise, chemical and radioactive material, and pathogenic and biological material. These natural and technological hazards can be further classified into non-mutual exclusive sets that can be partially addressed by geospatial science techniques. Institutions have also had to consider acts of human-induced terrorism in various forms and how to recover from a potential incident.

Natural Hazards

Floods. Flood hazards affect millions of people, and flood damages in the United States cost $470,000 to $682.3 million per year (FEMA, 2004). Flooding can develop slowly, manifest itself as flash floods, or become torrents due to the failure of water structures, such as a levee or dam.

Tornadoes. Many institutions of higher learning are located in tornado-prone areas. These violent storms can destroy infrastructure, disrupt communications, prevent normal modes of transportation, interfere with utilities, and cause fatalities. Every state has experienced tornadoes within the past several decades (National Climactic Data Center, 2008).

Hurricanes. Hurricanes that affect North America are initiated by extremely low-pressure tropical cyclonic activity that seasonally reaches coastlines. The intense storms cause catastrophic damage, not only at the coastline but several hundred miles inland. Hurricanes produce winds ranging from 74 to greater than 155 miles per hour and cause storm surges that range from four to over eighteen feet (FEMA, 2004). These storms can completely shut down educational institutions for months to years.

Extreme Temperatures. Extreme temperature changes, both cold and hot, can adversely affect the ability of educational institutions to perform at their optimum level. Extreme cold continues to have adverse affects on educational institutions in the forms of downed power lines, destroyed or frozen infrastructure, and human and animal hypothermia. Extreme cold can also trigger storm surges, thunderstorms, lightning, flooding, and the closure of schools for days at a time. Extreme heat can cause exposure, cramps, heat exhaustion, heatstroke or sunstroke, and even death. Heat waves can be responsible for increased ozone production, a reduction in plant photosynthesis, and urban heat islands.

Earthquakes. A large majority of the United States has seismic activity, some of which results in earthquakes and some severe aftershocks. Earthquakes are measured by the amount of energy released, commonly by the Richter magnitude scale. Earthquakes of mid to high magnitudes can cause moderate to devastating damage, as well as loss of life, at universities and colleges that lie near active seismic hazard areas (U.S. Geological Survey [USGS], 2006). Earthquakes underneath the world's oceans can also cause tsunamis that produce immense waves that have caused havoc with coastal institutions. Tsunami flood water can penetrate inland several miles, causing loss of property and life.

Volcanoes. Volcanic activity is currently limited to Hawaii, the Pacific coastline, and Alaska. Some of the hazards from volcanoes are extreme heat from molten rock or lava and pyroclastic flows, ash fallout that can travel for hundreds of miles, toxic gases, and ancillary hazards such as fires, landslides and mudflows, and destruction of property and lives (FEMA, 2004).

Landslides. Following intense rainfall periods, certain areas of the United States with unstable saturated soils produce gravity-driven landslides, mudslides, and debris slides. These dangerous slides can travel several miles from their origin, causing destruction of property and loss of life. Landslides can also be initiated by intense storms, fires, earthquake and volcanic activity, liquefaction, and poor land use practices by humans. Landslides can disrupt higher education institutions, and cause loss of infrastructure and lives.

Fire. Fires cause the deaths of more than four thousand and the injuring of over twenty-five thousand people in the United States annually. Property damage has been estimated to exceed over $8 billion annually as of 2004. Asphyxiation is the primary cause of these fatalities and injuries, even beyond those of burns (FEMA, 2004). Fires can cause destruction at institutions, disrupt normal campus activity, and cause injury and loss of life.

Health-Related Epidemics. Health-related issues are an ongoing issue for higher education institutions that admit students from all over the world. Natural epidemics and diseases such as meningitis, hepatitis, influenza, HIV/AIDS, sexually transmitted diseases, tuberculosis, cholera, yellow fever, dengue fever, smallpox, polio, and the various diseases classified by the Centers for Disease Control and Prevention are forcing institutions to be vigilant against these epidemics and outbreaks.

Technological Hazards

Information Technology. Universities and similar institutions are centers for advancing knowledge and technological innovations. Due to the very nature of sharing and publishing information data, some institutions possess open access to hardware, software, data, and information technology. Depending on the level of sophistication, institutions experience commonly occurring disasters such as power outages, hardware and software failure, human error and accidents, and technological malfunctions. Typically most institutions attempt to protect their information technology by establishing secure passwords, encryption algorithms, backup strategies, auxiliary power systems, and disaster recovery plans. Hawkins, Yen, and Chou (2000) document these disasters and their recovery procedures in the private sector. Unfortunately not all students, staff, and visitors follow the tenets and rules of information security, causing undesired consequences like privacy invasions, release of confidential data, malicious behavior, institution-wide crashes, vandalism, computer viruses, and other costly losses.

Chemical and Radioactive Material. Scientific educational institutions use different forms of chemicals and radioactive material for laboratories and advanced study in their respective fields. Many universities have set policies, safety regulations, and best practices for the handling, inspection, permitting, and waste management of chemical and biological material (Environmental, Health and Safety Policy Committee, 1995). But even with strict procedures and regulations, hazardous situations can occur in the laboratories, in improper storage vessels, during transportation, and during disposal. These materials have been known to cause respiratory difficulties, irritation to the senses, epidermal damage, more serious internal damage, and death (FEMA, 2004).

Pathogenic and Biological Material. The biological sciences taught at institutions routinely study and experiment with material that has a potential for release outside its intended environment. Valcik (2005) has described one university's policies and practices on the use, storage policies, and removal of these hazardous materials. Despite all efforts to contain and properly dispose of these materials, there exists the potential for introduction into the human body. Ingestion of these materials can result in illness and death if the immune system is unable to defend itself from the agent. Some examples of these living organisms are fungi, bacteria, protozoan, and viruses.

Human-Induced Hazards. Higher educational institutions have been plagued with the same human-induced hazards as the rest of society. As a microcosm of society, these institutions have reported rape, weapon offenses, sexual assault, harassment, underage alcohol consumption, illegal drug use, terrorism, firearm crimes, and many other crimes too numerous to list. As of 1991 it appears that school shootings, often accompanied by suicide, are on the rise (see Table 6.1 and Figure 6.1).

Institutions have had to evolve from the guard or watchman system begun in 1894 to a modern system using law enforcement officers who have full police powers (Sloan, 1992).

New Directions for Institutional Research • DOI: 10.1002/ir

Table 6.1. Institutional Killings and Locations

University or Research Center	City	State	Incident	Number Killed	Year
University of Texas at Austin	Austin	Texas	Shooting	17	1966
South Carolina State University	Orangeburg	South Carolina	Riot	3	1968
Harvard University	Cambridge	Massachusetts	Bombing	0	1970
Kent State University	Kent	Ohio	Riot	4	1970
Jackson State University	Jackson	Mississippi	Riot	2	1970
California State University	Fullerton	California	Shooting	7	1976
Florida State University	Tallahassee	Florida	Serial	2	1978
University of Utah	Salt Lake City	Utah	Bombing	0	1981
University of Iowa	Iowa City	Iowa	Shooting	6	1991
Simon's Rock College of Bard	Great Barrington	Massachusetts	Shooting	2	1992
University of North Carolina	Chapel Hill	North Carolina	Shooting	1	1995
San Diego State University	San Diego	California	Shooting	3	1996
Penn State University	University Park	Pennsylvania	Shooting	1	1996
University of Arkansas	Fayetteville	Arkansas	Shooting	2	2000
University of Virginia Appalachian	Grundy	Virginia	Shooting	3	2002
University of Arizona	Tucson	Arizona	Shooting	4	2002
Case Western Reserve	Cleveland	Ohio	Shooting	1	2003
Fairleigh Dickinson University	Florham Park	New Jersey	Shooting	2	2004
Shepherd University	Shepherdstown	West Virginia	Shooting	3	2006
Virginia Tech University	Blacksburg	Virginia	Shooting	32	2007
University of Washington	Seattle	Washington	Shooting	2	2007
Delaware State University	Dover	Delaware	Shooting	1	2007
Northern Illinois University	DeKalb	Illinois	Shooting	6	2008
South Mountain Community College	Phoenix	Arizona	Shooting	3	2008
Louisiana Technical College	Baton Rouge	Louisiana	Shooting	4	2008
University of Central Arkansas	Conway	Arkansas	Shooting	2	2008
Henry Ford Community College	Dearborn	Michigan	Shooting	2	2009
Hampton University	Hampton	Virginia	Shooting	0	2009

Source: www.wikipedia.org.

Figure 6.1. Location of Institutional Deaths from Shootings and Other Violence, by Year

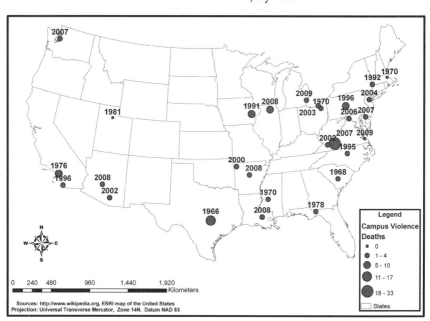

Initiation of Homeland Security and Emergency Management

Institutions of higher learning began to reconsider their policing requirements during the 1960s and 1970s as a result of the unrest and riots during the civil rights and antiwar protests. The rise in institutional crime during the past decades has led to a larger and more professional law enforcement cadre equal to or surpassing that of smaller municipalities (Ray, 1991). Following the September 11, 2001, terrorist attacks, FEMA (2003) published *Building a Disaster-Resistant University*, spelling out methods to organize resources and stakeholders, identify hazards and risks, produce a mitigation plan, and manage and implement the plan. This FEMA document bolstered the ability of higher education institutions to develop and publish their own emergency operation plans.

FEMA's (2003) *Building a Disaster-Resistant University* specifically states that maps should be used to identify hazards, inventory campus assets, and draw on the help of academic programs that have an expertise in mapping. In the public sector, most large municipalities take advantage of GIS, or some other form of geospatial sciences, to assist in their daily operations and emergency management (Cutter, 2003; Salkin, 2005). A review of selected institutions' emergency operation plans reveals an absence of GIS and little or no use of any geospatial techniques other than the campus map. Florida Agricultural and Mechanical University's "Emergency Contingency and Continuity of Operations Plan" (2005) is a comprehensive plan, yet lacks any mention of GIS or mapping. The University of Utah's "Emergency Operations Plan" (Blodgett, 2008) fails to take advantage of its quite extraordinary geography department's geospatial and hazard expertise. Utah has plans to receive grants from FEMA to produce a predisaster mitigation plan over a two-year period (Blodgett, 2008). Many universities have teamed up with local emergency responders, such as local police departments, sheriff's departments, and state law enforcement agencies, when their own resources become overwhelmed.

Universities That Utilize GIS for Homeland Security and Emergency Management

The use of GIS in institutional emergency management is a relatively new practice. Johnson (2003) describes a GIS emergency management system (GEMS) as an interactive system used at the University of Redlands emergency operation center. The GEMS contains a population locator component, a disaster occurrence component, and a query and analysis component. This system allows a rapid response because GIS data become readily available to first responders.

The conversion of available computer-aided design (CAD) files into a GIS for the purpose of emergency planning and response at Western Washington University is currently being prototyped for emergency responders (Lindeman, 2007). This prototype system converts CAD files, which currently are developed and maintained by the facilities division, to provide additional tabular data and possible spatial components. These GIS files can then be used in an emergency event.

At Pennsylvania State University, a geocollaborative crisis management system is being built to leverage the current office of physical plant (OPP), the local council of governments, the campus emergency coordinator, and the geography department's geospatial science GeoVista Center. This collaborative creates a process that uses GIS base map layers and attributes information and the conversion of OPP, allowing work groups at different locations to manage an incident (MacEachren and others, 2005). The system architecture is being enhanced with speech and gesture user interfaces that make it easier for decision makers to communicate with the GeoCollaborative Crisis Management system (Brewer, 2002).

How Institutions Can Use GIS for Homeland Security and Emergency Management

Institutional facilities information in the form of drawings, CAD files, and campus maps has been produced at every university. These data can be, and sometimes are, transformed into digital GIS databases for funding opportunities, university space and planning use, reporting facilities data to governmental entities, recruitment of students, and day-to-day operations and maintenance (Valcik, 2007). Johnson (2003), Lindeman (2007), and MacEachren and others (2005) have demonstrated that these facilities data can be input and transformed into layers that form the base map features comprising the beginning of an emergency management GIS. As referenced by the private and governmental sectors, the base map layers can be supplemented by global positional satellite data (Johnson and Davenhall, 2005), georeferenced digital images (Kafatos and others, 2002), and geostatistical analysis (Dubois, Pebesma, and Bossew, 2007). Obtaining ancillary GIS data from local governments, councils of governments, and other GIS entities would augment the base maps by expanding the areal dimensions that any emergency incident would include. Murchison (2003) and Galloway (2003) describe the mapping needs that first responders desired during the September 11, 2001, terrorist attack. These responders needed to know where to close and open transportation arteries, where to turn off and on public utilities, where to take the injured, where supplies and services can be distributed, and where objects and materials that can be harmful or fatal are stored. GIS can become an essential component in a rapid response system to answer these questions at educational institutions.

The safety of institutions depends on the accuracy of the GIS data, the availability of the data, and integrating this GIS data into disparate systems such as computer-aided dispatch, weather services, and other university-wide enterprise systems. This is known as situational awareness. These combinations of data provide what Environmental Systems Research Institute (ESRI, 2008) calls GIS situational awareness taxonomy. *GIS situational awareness taxonomy* is the term for obtaining base map, environmental, infrastructure, transportation, sensor, analytical tool, crime, information technology data, and interfacing capabilities. The ability to integrate the GIS situational awareness taxonomic data into a computing system that can be accessed by all groups and levels of responders is the way to achieve more-informed decision making choices for any emergency (Radke and others, 2000).

Why Higher Education Lags in the Use of GIS for Homeland Security and Emergency Management

There are two basic reasons for universities' lag in using GIS information.

Difficult Technology to Learn. Geographic information systems have a high learning curve (Jessop, 2004). It usually takes several months to years to master the complex and intricate fundamental concepts of geographic information systems and their differences from other types of information systems. Most GIS analysts have college degrees or several years of experience and on-the-job training to keep current in this quickly evolving discipline. The GIS Certification Institute, developed by the pioneering work of Obermeyer (1993), offers Certification in Geographic Information Systems (GISPs). Professionals (GISPs) must demonstrate proficiency in the areas of educational achievement, professional experience, and contributions to the profession. As of February 25, 2009, there were 4,386 GISPs certified worldwide.

It is likely that the majority of campus first responders will not be familiar with GIS and will probably resist using it during an incident (Cutter, 2003). GIS practitioners will have to train campus police, support staff, and administrative personnel in the correct use and distribution of data. Bromley and Reaves (1998) argue that campus police salaries for comparable positions in municipalities are lower. This salary disincentive and campus police educational requirements make adoption of GIS technologies more difficult due to their complexity. Universities, unlike municipalities, probably have not made the capital investment in a fully functional emergency operations center (EOC). These expensive centers with automated dispatch for fire, police, and ambulance service are not typically located on higher education institutions.

Expensive Technology. Initial investments in GIS hardware, software, implementation, training, and additional information technology support are high. University budgets are tightly monitored and controlled by the university administration and, for public institutions, their states. It is likely that initial investment in a GIS emergency management system is not a high-priority expenditure. Moreover, GIS data need to be constantly updated for accuracy, quality controlled, and integrated. This updating and monitoring of the system need full-time staff to keep it viable (Sommers, 2001). This additional expenditure may exceed even the most monetarily flexible institutions, as it may be difficult to find knowledgeable and experienced GIS staff to undertake such a project.

How GIS Professionals Can Make GIS a Viable Option for Higher Education Institutions

The responsibility of GIS professionals is to construct simple interfaces that are easily understood by campus police, first responders, and the users of the GIS for institutional emergency management. It has already been established what information should be provided to the users during an emergency (ESRI, 2008). The sources of the data should be delivered to users in a format that is easily comprehended and manipulated with little training. The bulk of the behind-the-scenes work in collecting, transforming, georectifying, analyzing, and maintaining these data will fall to the GIS analysts. During a crisis, Galloway (2003) suggested that first responders preferred paper maps, not digital amps or screen observations. The job of GIS professionals is to deliver the users simple, accurate, easily comprehended, and useful spatial information in the fastest way possible.

The examples of higher education institutions that are currently using GIS for emergency management have written specialized applications that conform to these requirements. These applications will reduce the learning curve and time spent in training.

In addition, institutions must be educated that GIS emergency technology will not be cost prohibitive. Most higher education institutions already have invested in an information technology and computer infrastructure. Many others have also invested in GIS and the geospatial sciences, as well as the ancillary equipment that works in conjunction with these technologies (Teodorescu, 2003). These assets are the building blocks that can be used to initiate a geocentric emergency management plan. Cutter (2003) has argued that building a GIS emergency system during or immediately after a disastrous event poses an almost insurmountable task because data and computer software and hardware are pieced together in an ad hoc manner that increases the time and cost for useful analysis.

Higher education institutions have faculty who are knowledgeable in the utility of GIS and geospatial technology. The faculty and their research assistants are capable of supporting a GIS initiative that can prepare for, respond to, recover from, and mitigate crisis events.

Conclusion

GIS and geospatial technology have proven to be an asset in emergency management situations (Kafatos, and others, 2002; Cahan and Ball, 2002; Galloway, 2003; Dubois, Pebesma, and Bossew, 2007). Sufficient data need to be collected and properly processed into a distributive computing system that authorities can access. This GIS homeland security and emergency management system for higher education institutions can address and assist in responding to any natural, technological, or human-induced hazard. Given that almost every incident that occurs on a university campus has a spatial component, GIS and geospatial technologies are ideal for allowing a university to address, analyze, and assist administrators in making correct decisions. Whether disasters are caused by natural forces, computer or network externalities, or some act that humans initiate, the ultimate question remains: Can institutions react in time to save infrastructure and lives? The benefits of using GIS for institutional emergencies far outweigh the alternatives.

References

Aitken, S. C., and Michel, S. M. "Who Contrives the 'Real' in GIS? Geographic Information, Planning and Critical Theory." *Cartography and Geographic Information Systems*, 2007, 22(1), 17–29.
Blodgett, J. "Planning for a Disaster-Resistant U." *Continuum*, 2008, *18*(2), 6.

Brewer, I. "Cognitive Systems Engineering and GIScience: Lessons Learned from a Work Domain Analysis for the Design of a Collaborative, Multimodal Emergency Management GIS." Geographic Information Science, Second International Conference, Boulder, Colo., Sept. 25–28, 2002.

Bromley, M. L., and Reaves, B. A. "Comparing Campus and Municipal Police: The Human Resource Dimension." Policing: An International Journal of Police Strategies and Management, 1998, 21, 534–546.

Cahan, B., and Ball, M. "GIS at Ground Zero: Spatial Technology Bolsters World Trade Center Response and Recovery." GEOWorld, 2002, 15(1), 26–29.

Chrisman, N. R. "What Does 'GIS' Mean?" Transactions in GIS, 1999, 3, 175–186.

Cutter, S. L. "GI Science, Disasters, and Emergency Management." Transactions in GIS, 2003, 7, 439–445.

Dubois, G., Pebesma, E. J., and Bossew, P. "Automatic Mapping in Emergency: A Geostatistical Perspective." International Journal of Emergency Management, 2007, 4, 455–467.

Environmental, Health and Safety Policy Committee. Responsibility for Environmental, Health and Safety. Berkeley: University of California, 1995.

Environmental Systems Research Institute (ESRI). "Public Safety and Homeland Security Situational Awareness." Redlands, Calif.: ESRI, Feb. 2008. Retrieved Feb. 5, 2009, from http://www.esri.com/library/whitepapers/pdfs/situational-awareness.pdf.

Federal Emergency Management Agency (FEMA). Building a Disaster-Resistant University. Washington, D.C.: U.S. Government Printing Office, 2003.

Federal Emergency Management Agency (FEMA). Are You Ready? An In-Depth Guide to Citizen Preparedness. Washington, D.C.: U.S. Government Printing Office, 2004.

Florida Agricultural and Mechanical University. "Emergency Contingency and Continuity of Operations Plan." 2005. Retrieved Jan. 13, 2010, from http://www.onyxsphere.com/famuehsd/doc/ecp_2005-07-27v2.doc.

Galloway, G. E. "Emergency Preparedness and Response: Lessons Learned from 9/11." In S. L. Cutter, D. B. Richardson, and T. J. Wilbanks (eds.), Geographical Dimensions of Terrorism. New York: Routledge, 2003.

Hawkins, S. E., Yen, D. C., and Chou, D. C. "Disaster Recovery Planning: A Strategy for Data Security." Information Management & Computer Security, 2000, 8, 222–229.

Jessop, M. "The Visualization of Spatial Data in the Humanities." Literary and Linguistic Computing, 2004, 19, 335–350.

Johnson, K. "GIS Emergency Management for the University of Redlands." Unpublished paper, 2003.

Johnson, R., and Davenhall, B. "Improving Emergency Planning and Response with Geographic Information Systems." Redlands, Calif.: ESRI, 2005. Retrieved Mar. 29, 2009, from http://www.esri.com/library/whitepapers/pdfs/emergency-planning-response.pdf.

Kafatos, M., and others. "Utilizing Remote Sensing Data in a Quick Response System." In Pecora 15/Land Satellite Information IV/ISPRS Commission I/FIEOS 2002 Conference Proceedings, 2002.

Lindeman, C. "Development of a Prototype GIS Utilizing CAD Data for Emergency Planning and Response, Western Washington University." 2007. Retrieved Mar. 29, 2009, from http://deptweb.wwu.edu/huxley/huxweb/gis/EGEO452/07_projects/Lindeman.

MacEachren, A. M., and others. "Project Highlight: GeoCollaborative Crisis Management." In Proceedings of the 2005 National Conference on Digital Government Research, Atlanta, Ga, May 15–18, 2005.

Murchison, S. B. Saving Time, Lives with Integrated Data. Los Gatos, Calif.: Government West, May–June 2003.

National Climatic Data Center. U.S. Tornado Climatology. Washington, D.C.: NOAA, 2008.

Obermeyer, N. "Certifying GIS Professionals: Challenges and Alternatives." *URISA Journal*, 1993, *5*, 67–75.

Radke, J., and others. "Application Challenges for Geographic Information Science: Implications for Research, Education, and Policy for Emergency Preparedness and Response." *URISA Journal*, 2000, *12*(2), 15–30.

Ray, G. "Campus Police: A Different View." *FBI Law Enforcement Bulletin*, 1991, *60*(5), 14–15.

Salkin, P. E. "GIS in an Age of Homeland Security: Accessing Public Information to Ensure a Sustainable Environment." *William and Mary Environmental Law and Policy Review*, 2005, *30*, 55–94.

Sloan, J. J. "Modern Campus Police: An Analysis of Their Evolution, Structure, and Function." *American Journal of Police*, 1992, *11*(2), 85–104.

Sommers, R. *Quick Guide to GIS Implementation and Management.* Des Plaines, Ill.: URISA Press, 2001.

Teodorescu, D. (ed.). *Using Geographic Information Systems in Institutional Research.* New Directions for Institutional Research, no. 120. San Francisco: Jossey-Bass, 2003.

U.S. Geological Survey (USGS). "Earthquake Hazards—A National Threat, Fact Sheet 2006-3016." 2006.

Valcik, N. "The Logistical Tracking System (LTS) Five Years Later: What Have We Learned?" In N. Valcik (ed.), *Space: The Final Frontier for Institutional Research.* New Directions for Institutional Research, no. 140. San Francisco: Jossey-Bass, 2007.

Valcik, N. A. "The Protection of Physical Assets in Research Universities for Biological HAZMAT: Policies, Practices and Improvements." Unpublished doctoral dissertation, University of Texas at Dallas, 2005.

STUART B. MURCHISON, Ph.D, C.P., GISP, is a clinical associate professor of geography and geospatial sciences at The University of Texas at Dallas.

NEW DIRECTIONS FOR INSTITUTIONAL RESEARCH • DOI: 10.1002/ir

7

This chapter discusses new guidelines for chemical hazardous materials for homeland security compliance and the role institutional research has in these compliance mandates.

Compliance Issues and Homeland Security With New Federal Regulations for Higher Education Institutions

Nicolas A. Valcik

Since the Manhattan Project in the early 1940s, higher education institutions have increasingly required more advanced research resources—facilities, personnel, equipment, and materials—to explore new areas of science for mankind's advancement. Concurrently, controlled substances such as lysergic acid diethylamide (LSD) were beginning to be researched to determine the effects on the brain (Becker, Geer, Riesman, and Weiss, 1968). As stated by Howard S. Becker: "In the early 1960s, Timothy Leary, Richard Alpert and others began using it with normal subjects as a means of 'conscious expansion.' Their work received a great deal of publicity, particularly after a dispute with Harvard authorities over its potential danger" (Becker, Geer, Riesman, and Weiss, 1968, p. 273).

Research advancements into different fields of study have increased the risks for accidents, criminal acts, or a potential breach of national security, and the types of hazardous materials (HAZMAT) stored and used at universities and colleges are under new scrutiny. Before, a chemistry laboratory might only have basic substances such as sulfur, iodine, and magnesium. Today, a well-equipped research laboratory can stock anything from morphine and other controlled substances to hydrochloric acid and other extremely corrosive materials. Since the 1940s, additional federal, state, and local guidelines have been implemented to broaden

NEW DIRECTIONS FOR INSTITUTIONAL RESEARCH, no. 146, Summer 2010 © Wiley Periodicals, Inc.
Published online in Wiley InterScience (www.interscience.wiley.com) • DOI: 10.1002/ir.345

oversight of universities' research activities in an effort to promote a greater sense of security and safety for the general public.

This chapter examines how higher education institutions are affected by compliance, safety, and security issues and how institutional research can play a role in chemical HAZMAT control. Particular emphasis is placed on the impact of the Department of Homeland Security Appropriations Act of 2007: Section 550, DHS-2006–0073, RIN 1601-AA41, 6 CFR Part 27—Chemical Facility Anti-Terrorism Standards (Department of Homeland Security, 2007). To illustrate the importance of, and the challenges involved in, complying with Homeland Security's new chemical guidelines, this chapter also includes a synopsis of an in-depth case study conducted at a higher education institution.

Definition of HAZMAT

To understand why the federal government is so concerned about the regulation of HAZMAT, it is important to define what constitutes HAZMAT. Southern California Edison, one of the largest electric utilities in the United States and the largest subsidiary of Edison International, defines HAZMAT as both a material and as a by-product (Southern California Edison, 2008):

> Hazardous Material: Any material that because of its quantity, concentration, or physical or chemical characteristics, poses a significant present or potential hazard to human health and safety or to the environment if released into the workplace or the environment. Hazardous materials include, but are not limited to, hazardous substances, hazardous waste, and any material which a handler or the administering regulatory agency has a reasonable basis for believing would be injurious to the health and safety of persons or harmful to the environment if released into the workplace or the environment (California Health and Safety Code, Section 25501 [o]). A number of properties may cause a substance to be considered hazardous, including toxicity, ignitibility, corrosivity, or reactivity.
>
> Hazardous Waste: A waste or combination of waste which because of its quantity, concentration, or physical, chemical, or infection characteristics, may cause or significantly contribute to an increase in mortality or an increase in serious irreversible or incapacitation-reversible illness; or pose a substantial present or potential hazard to human health or the environment, due to factors including, but not limited to, carcinogenicity, acute toxicity, chronic toxicity, bioaccumulative properties, or persistence in the environment, when improperly treated, stored, transported, or disposed of or otherwise managed (California Health and Safety Code, Section 25141). California waste identification and classification regulations are found in Title 22 of the California Code of Regulations.

The four main categories of HAZMAT are chemical, biological, radiation and waste.

The focus of this chapter is on chemical HAZMAT since it is these substances that are under increased scrutiny by the federal government. Chemical HAZMAT is now regulated under the new guidelines set by the Department of Homeland Security (DHS). Chemicals that are considered controlled substances also fall under the jurisdiction of the Drug Enforcement Agency (DEA). Furthermore, waste produced from research and operational activities must be disposed according to Environmental Protection Agency (EPA) regulations. Chemical HAZMAT issues can have a great impact on campus security and first responders' ability to contain an emergency situation.

Institutional Research and HAZMAT Compliance

Most institutional research offices are responsible for federal and state reporting, and it is within this area of influence that a university's handling of chemical HAZMAT intersects with the institutional research office's efforts to fulfill their reporting duties. Many institutional research offices are uniquely positioned to assist with facilities and HAZMAT reporting because such offices are designed to deliver federal and state reports in a timely and accurate manner, are accustomed to working with information technology systems, and occasionally serve on university committees that encompass many areas, including facilities. Key reports concerning research facilities that are already under the purview of institutional research are facilities inventory reports, indirect cost studies, and National Science Foundation surveys, to name a few. Therefore, if a university is interested in developing a means to track and report chemical HAZMAT, its institutional research office can be a valuable asset as it works toward achieving such a goal.

At The University of Texas at Dallas, facilities and HAZMAT issues were addressed through the development of the logistical tracking system (LTS). This system functioned to account for facility square footage to satisfy indirect cost study reports and facility inventory reports. This system was later expanded to provide support services for environmental health and safety (EHS), the University Police Department, and a variety of other business affairs departments. Developing LTS required an understanding of federal and state statutes, local requirements (for example, of the local fire departments), the institution's operational requirements, and where data (such as human resources data) could be obtained and imported into LTS. In addition, the application required a new approach to integrating existing business processes as opposed to the traditional method of relegating processes into silos managed individually by departments.

Similar solutions can be found for other universities. Interaction among various departments is essential to achieving both common and

NEW DIRECTIONS FOR INSTITUTIONAL RESEARCH • DOI: 10.1002/ir

tangential goals. An institutional research office, by virtue of its unique organizational position, can be instrumental in linking these departments by tapping into the various university databases that it uses for reporting and research. For example, an institutional research office must mine financial, human resource, and facilities databases to complete indirect cost reports. With its holistic perspective on university operations and its understanding of compliance issues, an institutional research office can become a crucial keystone in a university's efforts toward diminishing risks and improving HAZMAT controls.

Database Content

What type of data can an institutional research office gather to assist operations with homeland security and emergency management issues? At "The University," the strategic planning office assisted various departments by developing and providing a facilities tracking application (LTS) and extracting data on facilities, research contracts and grants, and personnel assignments from the main computer system and linking the data to security infrastructure and HAZMAT supplies and locations provided by the environmental health and safety (EHS) department. The strategic planning office linked facilities data (such as building and room information) to each container of HAZMAT recorded in the EHS department's inventory, thus providing an accurate depiction of HAZMAT status by type, location, room type, and departmental ownership.

HAZMAT data can be expanded with information extracted from the financial reporting system, particularly contracts and grants, and linked to the facilities data to determine ownership of HAZMAT through the principal investigator assigned to the research space. Identifying the principal investigator helps in determining who is responsible for safety and inventory control within a particular area. In addition, human resource data contain faculty and staff information by building and room assignment. Linking employee room assignment data to existing facility and HAZMAT inventory data enabled "The University" to accurately determine the numbers and locations of personnel in the event of an evacuation or other emergency.

Government Regulation of Chemical HAZMAT

It is important to track chemical HAZMAT primarily because all higher education institutions must be in compliance with federal, state, and local statutes and ordinances. Repercussions from noncompliance can include anything from funding cuts and fines to criminal charges. New federal guidelines such as the PATRIOT Act 2001, Bioterrorism Preparedness and Response Act of 2002, and Homeland Security Chemical Facility Anti-Terrorism Standards 2007 statutes all impact the research activities at universities. Second, with recent attention brought to homeland security issues, higher education institutions that have active research programs contain a wealth of chemicals that can be used for terrorism or for other criminal purposes. How responsive higher education institutions are to the current homeland security initiatives is still debated. Recently the University of Texas at Austin was accused of ignoring shortfalls in safety and federal compliance guidelines by a former employee who was a veteran national security expert (Associated Press, 2008). As can be seen in Figure 7.1 and Figure 7.2, which maps several major HAZMAT incidents, the HAZMAT incidents tend to be more concentrated in certain parts of the United States.

The federal government maintains an interest in how universities manage chemical HAZMAT because chemicals used in traditional research laboratories can be stolen and used to commit crimes or acts of terrorism. Since some higher education institutions use controlled substances like morphine and LSD in animal research, the Drug Enforcement Agency (DEA) maintains strict regulation on these types of controlled substances. New statutes from Homeland Security categorize certain chemicals as potential danger for release, theft or diversion or sabotage, or contamination, and these chemicals are denoted as "chemicals of interest" if the

Figure 7.1. 1951 to 2009 HAZMAT Incidents in U.S. Higher Education Institutions and Government Research Centers

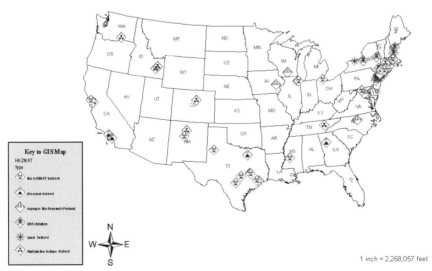

Sources: Barat (2005), Campus Consortium for Environmental Excellence (2000), Christensen (2009), CIDRAP (2008), EPA (2002, 2008), Hilfinger (2009), Mount Holyoke College (1996), Oklahoma Higher Education (2000), Powers (2007), Robins (2007), Ryder and Gandsman (1995), Schnirring (2007), Simpson (2009), Sunshine Project (2007), University of Maine (2004), Valcik (2006), Vasich (2002), Wikipedia (2009).

NEW DIRECTIONS FOR INSTITUTIONAL RESEARCH • DOI: 10.1002/ir

Figure 7.2. 1951 to 2009 HAZMAT Incidents in the Northeast at U.S. Higher Education Institutions and Government Research Centers

Sources: Barat (2005), Campus Consortium for Environmental Excellence (2000), Christensen (2009), CIDRAP (2008), EPA (2002, 2008), Hilfinger (2009), Mount Holyoke College (1996), Oklahoma Higher Education (2000), Powers (2007), Robins (2007), Ryder and Gandsman (1995), Schnirring (2007), Simpson (2009), Sunshine Project (2007), University of Maine (2004), Valcik (2006), Vasich (2002), Wikipedia (2009).

amount of the chemicals is above a threshold limit at a facility (Department of Homeland Security, 2007).

According to DHS guidelines, the following chemicals must be reported: chlorine (1,875 pounds threshold limit), chloroform (15,000 pounds threshold limit), mercury fulminate (2,000 pounds threshold limit), and nitrogen trioxide (any amount threshold limit). These chemicals are only a sample of what can be found at higher education institutions that are also listed on the DHS chemicals of interest appendix. (Chapter Two in this volume addresses changes in higher education culture with regard to the new homeland security initiatives.)

In the past, data on HAZMAT used and stored at universities might have been recorded on paper, if at all. Given the preponderance of HAZMAT on most university property and the increasing complexity of federal reporting mandates, the decision to record this information electronically seems to be the most sound. An electronic database can be accessed readily by first responders in times of crises, can be restricted by information security personnel so that only individuals with proper clearance can access the data, and can enable environmental health personnel to track HAZMAT across the university to exact locations or individuals. However, once HAZMAT information is recorded electronically, information security and risk assessment take on much greater importance. As stated by Texas Administrative Code, Title 1—Administration, Part 10—Department of Information Resources, Chapter 202 Information Security Standards, Subsection C—Security Standards for Institutions of Higher Education, Rule §202.72, managing security risks:

(1) High Risk-annual assessment–Information resources that;
  (A) Involve large dollar amounts or significantly important transactions, such that business or government processes would be hindered or an impact on public health or safety would occur if the transactions were not processed timely and accurately, or
  (B) Contain confidential or sensitive data such that unauthorized disclosure would cause real damage to the parties involved, or
  (C) Impact a large number of people or interconnected systems. [State of Texas, 2008]

According to this Texas statute, all information resources, inclusive of electronically recorded chemical HAZMAT data, must be secured and treated as high risk information. Chemical HAZMAT data can have an impact on transactions and processes, inflict damage, and impact large numbers of people or interconnected systems.

HAZMAT, including chemical HAZMAT, is also considered an asset to a public organization. For example, ammonium nitrate, a chemical widely used as a fertilizer, has monetary value, which requires that it be inventoried for cost considerations. Ammonium nitrate is also a dangerous chemical; when improperly used, it can become explosive, causing real harm to parties and disrupting key systems as it did in the bombing of the Oklahoma City Alfred P. Murrah Federal Building in 1995. Hence chemical HAZMAT itself, not just HAZMAT data, falls under Texas statute.

Risk Assessment: Chemical HAZMAT at Higher Education Institutions

The public health of the university community must be considered when assessing the risks associated with HAZMAT safety and security. These considerations provide ample reason to track HAZMAT to their locations and to secure HAZMAT properly. If a fire or a chemical disbursement occurs in a facility known or suspected to contain chemical HAZMAT, firefighters and other first responders will need to be informed of what those chemicals are to protect themselves and others and to contain the

NEW DIRECTIONS FOR INSTITUTIONAL RESEARCH • DOI: 10.1002/ir

emergency situation properly. A detailed and updated chemical inventory is necessary to ensure that first responders can correctly assess the threat potential of the situation, conduct proper evacuation procedures if necessary, employ adequate protective gear, and select the best methods for containing the emergency.

An emergency situation involving chemical HAZMAT should not be taken lightly. A typical research institution often uses and stores highly dangerous chemicals such as chlorine gas that have the potential to kill or injure people on a smaller scale. An extreme example of the potential destructive power of a large chemical release is the 1984 incident at Bhopal, India, where chemical exposure from a Union Carbide Plant killed approximately thirty-eight hundred people and injured several thousand more (Union Carbide, 2007). A smaller-scale event still retains the potential for death and injury to the campus community, as well as to residential and business areas that surround most universities. The case study university in this chapter is surrounded by a residential area that includes small businesses and public schools, which might necessitate a significant public evacuation in the event of a large-scale, airborne dispersal of dangerous toxins.

One challenge facing higher education institutions is the need to secure facilities while maintaining an open campus. Unlike national research laboratories such as Los Alamos, higher education institutions have other missions besides research that they must accomplish, such as instruction, public outreach programs, and medical services. The size of a typical college or university campus (or multiple campus locations), coupled with the fact that research and medical services are frequently in multiple facilities that have mixed uses, can make securing chemical HAZMAT extremely difficult. If an emergency does occur (such as a fire), safety concerns are also a bigger concern than if the HAZMAT was contained in just one or two buildings. In an effort to better secure their facilities, a number of campuses have begun to concentrate their research facilities in separate buildings. MIT, for example, has been relocating classified research away from its main campus to improve security (Campbell, 2002).

Over time, more agencies have become increasingly involved with HAZMAT regulation at higher education institutions. The Nuclear Regulatory Committee (NRC) is the primary agency concerned with regulating radioactive materials at higher education institutions. Agencies such as the Department of Transportation (DOT) and the Environmental Protection Agency (EPA) are primarily concerned with proper waste removal for higher education institutions. A number of universities have been fined heavily by the EPA for failure to remove waste properly (EPA, 2002, 2008; Valcik, 2006). Other federal agencies that have passed statutes and audited biological and/or chemical HAZMAT at higher education institutions include the National Institutes of Health (NIH), the Centers for Disease

Control and Prevention (CDC), the Department of Agriculture, and the Drug Enforcement Agency (DEA).

Currently research universities seem to be focused more on reacting to HAZMAT incidents than on developing proactive measures to increase security or safety. At Oklahoma State University, proper disposal and handling of HAZMAT and employee accountability for misconduct, fraud, or misuse of HAZMAT are addressed in the policy and procedures manual, but such issues as maintaining an inventory of certain substances, protection of certain items, or how to contend with particular items in case of an emergency are not addressed (Oklahoma State University, 1983). The University of Maine addresses protection and procedural controlled use for HAZMAT and has a provision for inventory control of controlled substances (University of Maine, 2004); however, the University of Maine does not require a centralized tracking of HAZMAT to locations and personnel. At Tulane University Health Sciences Center (2004), the Office of Environmental Health and Safety's document entitled "Hazardous Materials and Waste" seems more focused on proper disposal of HAZMAT than on security or inventory control.

The various biological safety and chemical safety practices for laboratories are typically focused more on laboratory safety than security or inventory control. At the University of Texas at Arlington, safety is the primary focus of the policies and procedures. Inventory control is vaguely referenced to "chemical inventory reporting procedures" (University of Texas at Arlington, 2004). At the University of New Brunswick, policies and procedures on laboratory safety state an inventory list shall be kept on all hazardous materials. The policies also are very specific on what types of containers are used for various HAZMAT situations (University of New Brunswick, 2004). Yale University has a specific section in its laboratory safety policies for lasers and centralized distribution of solvents (Yale University, 2004). Texas A&M University–Corpus Christi's policies on chemical laboratory safety focus primarily on safety issues (Texas A&M University–Corpus Christi, 2004). In short, the policies that have been reviewed lack detailed information on inventory control and security procedures for use, storage, transference, or transportation of chemical elements within the university environment.

Many issues regarding chemical HAZMAT safety practices could be rectified by adhering to a definitive federal standard or industry guideline. However, to date no standards have been uncovered that can definitively outline how to properly secure research laboratories and HAZMAT on university property. There are several possible explanations as to why no standards can be found. One explanation is that the security measures are classified and therefore would be unavailable for public consumption. Another explanation could be that due to the great variation in research efforts being conducted, it is difficult to craft one set of criteria that can satisfy all issues that might arise in any given situation, thus forcing each

NEW DIRECTIONS FOR INSTITUTIONAL RESEARCH • DOI: 10.1002/ir

organization to develop its own standards. The open access nature of college campuses can make securing most research buildings difficult unless
such buildings are located completely offsite. In addition, the age of some
research facilities might prevent necessary upgrades. For example, rewir-
ing a research laboratory that was built in the 1930s to accommodate electronic locks and surveillance cameras might be quite impossible due to the
lack of available crawl space. Therefore, best practices, defined as those
that best fit the organizational functionality, culture, and facilities, will
vary for each type of research within each type of facility. Purpura (1989)
has noted:

> Losses from crimes, fires, accidents, natural disasters and so forth, are the
> obvious problems. The strategies to counter these losses are numerous. A
> reader with even the slightest knowledge can list the more common ones:
> security officers, alarm systems, planning and preparation, and the like. It is
> the utmost importance, however, for practitioners to look beyond these
> basic strategies to new methods. A never-ending search for new and better
> ideas is a necessity in dealing with our complex, changing world (p. 6).

There is also the possibility that since securing HAZMAT is a new
concern, there has not yet been a centralized effort to develop operating
procedures for HAZMAT issues. Therefore, it appears that the best guidelines available are the Department of Homeland Security's Chemical Facility Anti-Terrorism Standards, which not only address the need to protect
HAZMAT areas and keep an accurate chemical inventory but have also
been written by a federal agency with extensive influence.

HAZMAT Security Assessment at the Case Study
University: Research Methodology

To research HAZMAT security issues in a higher education environment,
a public university was selected as a case study to illustrate standard practices regarding facility and laboratory security and HAZMAT handling. In
this study, the selected institution is referred to "The University," all
buildings have been given fictitious acronyms, and all personnel involved
in the study are designated by their employment category at "The University" with a number to conceal their identities. For the purposes of this
chapter, I will only disclose data for a small sample of the buildings surveyed: "NEECS," "SEECS," and "VS."

This research uses a case study format that utilizes grounded theory
as a starting basis for collecting data. Using unobtrusive observation techniques, data was gathered on four Sundays in 2004: May 2, May 9, May 16,
and May 23. Since most of "The University's" activities were dormant on
Sundays, this day was selected since access to buildings should have been

NEW DIRECTIONS FOR INSTITUTIONAL RESEARCH • DOI: 10.1002/ir

more restrictive compared with weekday access, and personnel and student traffic would be at the lowest levels. The working hypothesis was that research laboratories not in use would be locked down, thus securing the HAZMAT contained inside. In addition to unobtrusive observations, archival documentation, participant observer techniques, and interviews were used to triangulate research data.

To accomplish my unobtrusive observations, I was accompanied by the crime prevention coordinator on several security surveys. On the third security survey, I observed the crime prevention coordinator check access to research laboratories, inquire personnel as to whether they should be in the facility, and question faculty and students as to what types of specimens were kept in refrigerators. The crime prevention coordinator carried a radio but no visible identification that he was part of the campus security force. On three of the surveys, I carried a clipboard and camera and was dressed casually in a T-shirt, ball cap, and blue jean shorts. On the fourth security survey, the crime prevention coordinator wore a black shirt and black pants and was carrying a radio with no identification to indicate that he worked for campus security. I wore a pair of green army pants, a T-shirt, and a ball cap and was carrying a clipboard along with two cameras.

During all four security surveys I was not asked by anyone who I was or what I was doing in the facilities. On the third and fourth security surveys, the crime prevention coordinator was never asked who he was or why he was checking doors and asking questions about HAZMAT. During the third survey, I remained inside the facilities for over three hours unobserved and unchallenged by any university personnel, faculty, or student. At no time during the four security surveys did I encounter any police officers or police guards. Once I saw a police officer driving a patrol car around campus. A police officer who had apparently ended his shift did notice me driving into a parking lot but took no action.

Several of the main buildings on campus are connected by a series of skywalks. These buildings include a classroom building with several faculty offices, a mixed-use classroom and laboratory building with administrative offices, an engineering complex, a mixed-use arts and academic computing facility, and three science buildings, including one primarily devoted to chemistry. These skywalks are rarely locked, even during the weekend, and do not feature cameras or other surveillance equipment. Once inside any of these connected buildings, a person could literally walk from one end of campus to the other without going outside. Such a person would be able to access every major research facility and would have time to steal materials or equipment, vandalize, inflict bodily harm upon students or faculty who might be alone, detonate materials and so on. They would also be able to open loading dock gates from the inside to steal large consignments of HAZMAT materials or research laboratory equipment. Rooms that contained HAZMAT materials did not have

Material Safety Data Sheets (MSDS) lists posted on the doors, a clear viola-
tion of the Emergency Operation Plan (EOP).

Methodology. A rigorous content analysis was undertaken with this
research. I will summarize the multiple processes and procedures that I
took to ensure the accuracy of the qualitative data. (For a detailed explanation of the research methodology, see Valcik, 2006.)

First, I completed a series of unobtrusive surveys to determine the
existing state of HAZMAT conditions within "The University's" facilities.
To gather data for the unobtrusive surveys, I developed a checklist of
potential HAZMAT conditions that were common to all of the buildings
that I planned to investigate. I made every effort to maintain consistency
by following the same pathway through each building I entered and by
investigating each building during the same day of the week and similar
times of the day. I supplemented my surveys with digital photographs of
preexisting HAMZAT conditions.

Under the grounded theory, I accumulated archival data regarding
HAZMAT policies and procedures to gain insight into how HAZMAT conditions at "The University" had evolved over time. I then conducted interviews using a semi-structured method which allowed the respondents the
flexibility to provide more information if they so chose. I refrained from
using an electronic recording device and instead took handwritten notes
because I felt that given the sensitive nature of the subject matter, the
interviewees would not be so forthcoming with information if they were
being recorded. I selected my interviewees because they were a captive
audience (they were employees of "The University") or through the
"snowballing method" whereby I determined who to interview next based
on names mentioned during previous interviews.

The participant observer phase of my data collection allowed me to
fill any gaps in knowledge on "The University's" HAZMAT operations and
how conditions at "The University" evolved over time. As a participant
observer, I had an opportunity not only to gather important data through
my official connections but also to witness the resolution of many
HAZMAT issues that were present at "The University." These data collection methods enabled me to triangulate my data so that I obtained as complete and accurate a picture as possible on the evolution and conditions of
HAZMAT operations at "The University."

Unobtrusive Observations. To conduct a series of unobtrusive
observations, I asked "The University's" crime prevention coordinator to
accompany me on several surveys. The NEECS and SEECS buildings contain classrooms and research laboratories for the institution's engineering
programs. During the third security survey, I observed that all research
laboratories were locked and were accessible only through card reader
locks which were affixed to the doors. On the fourth security survey,
the crime prevention coordinator and I were not challenged by any faculty
or students present and were able to access the loading dock area. The

loading dock area had several flammable pressurized gas cylinders present, including oxygen and hydrogen gas cylinders (Figure 7.3). Two cameras were mounted in the loading dock area but were not operational (Figure 7.4). And the clean room that was accessible through an emergency exit had been left open. Behind the building, a liquid nitrogen tank was stored behind a fence surrounded by concrete pillars installed as partial protection from accidental collision.

On October 13, 2004, I was scheduled to interview Researcher No. 7 at the NEECS but was prevented from making my appointment because a large amount of chloroform had spilled at the entrance of the laboratory and the hallway corridor. I relocated my interview with Researcher No. 7 to the loading dock outside the NEECS building while the environmental safety department cleaned up the spill. For more details on HAZMAT Conditions at the NEECS and SEECS Buildings, please refer to Table 7.1.

VS is a stand-alone building that contains an art gallery and art studios (Table 7.2). According to Staff Member No. 10, the building was originally built as a barn to house tractors and lawn care equipment for the physical plant personnel and was never intended to be an art studio. This building stores numerous chemicals which are used in photography,

Figure 7.3.

Figure 7.4.

Table 7.1. HAZMAT Conditions at the NEECS and SEECS Buildings

Action	May 2	May 9	May 16	May 23
HAZMAT chemicals present	Yes	Yes	Yes	Yes
HAZMAT chemicals unsecured	Yes	Yes	Yes	Yes
Students present	Yes	Yes	Yes	Yes
External doors open or ajar	Yes	Yes	Yes	Yes
Internal laboratory door locks not working	Yes	Yes	Yes	Yes
Welder present	No	No	No	No
HAZMAT materials in open areas	Yes	Yes	Yes	Yes
Code key locks present	Yes	Yes	Yes	Yes
Code key lock door open	No	No	No	No
Faculty present	No	No	No	No
Researcher or crime coordinator challenged	No	No	No	No
HAZMAT materials labeled	Yes	Yes	Yes	Yes
Cameras present	Yes	Yes	Yes	Yes
Cameras monitored	No	No	No	No
Cameras operational	No	No	No	No
Security force member present	No	No	No	No

Table 7.2. HAZMAT Conditions at the VS Building

Action	May 2	May 9	May 16	May 23
HAZMAT chemicals present	Yes	Yes	Yes	Yes
HAZMAT chemicals unsecured	Yes	Yes	Yes	Yes
Students present	No	No	No	Yes
External doors open or ajar	Yes	Yes	Yes	Yes
External door locks not working	Yes	Yes	Yes	Yes
Welder present	Yes	Yes	Yes	Yes
HAZMAT materials in open areas	Yes	Yes	Yes	Yes
Code key locks present	Yes	Yes	Yes	Yes
Code key lock door open	No	No	Yes	No
Faculty present	No	No	No	No
Researcher or crime coordinator challenged	No	No	No	No
HAZMAT materials labeled	Yes	Yes	Yes	Yes
Cameras present	No	No	No	No
Cameras monitored	No	No	No	No
Cameras operational	No	No	No	No
Security force member present	No	No	No	No

metal working, ceramics, wood and stone sculpture, painting, and print-making. On the third security survey, I observed several HAZMAT containers stacked by the back door for disposal. These containers were still in the exact location on the fourth security survey. Since the back door is a main entrance into the facility, stacking HAZMAT near the door presents a safety issue. Twelve one-gallon containers of photo chemicals had been tagged for disposal and left out in the open (Figure 7.5).

In several of the art studios, chemicals such as lacquers were stored in an unlocked cabinet that was not fireproof. Chemicals such as mineral spirits and paints were kept in unsecured storage units (Figure 7.6). Two welders, a pressurized gas type and an arc welder, were in one of the workrooms. The welders were not secured and could be used to break into other facilities (Figure 7.7).

On the third and fourth security surveys, the building was unsecured because two doors by the side porch were propped open and the front door lock mechanism was not functional. On the fourth security survey, a student was working in a studio at 5:30 p.m. The facility was supposed to be inaccessible, but a door was propped open. The crime prevention coordinator asked the student to please lock the door when she completed her work. The student, who appeared rattled by our presence, responded that she had entered the building through the back door, which was unlocked. She eventually agreed to close the door when she left the building.

During the fourth security survey, the VS computer laboratory was found unlocked, and HAZMAT chemicals were present inside (Figure 7.8). The door had a code-key lock mechanism, but it was not a self-closing door. No cameras were in place at the entrances.

NEW DIRECTIONS FOR INSTITUTIONAL RESEARCH • DOI: 10.1002/ir

Figure 7.5.

Figure 7.6.

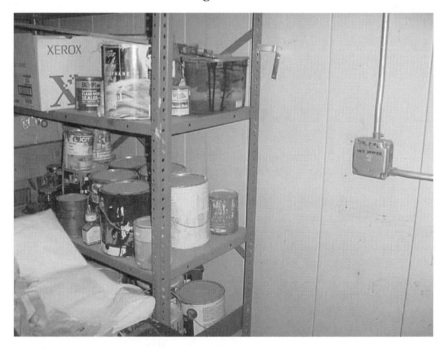

Figure 7.7.

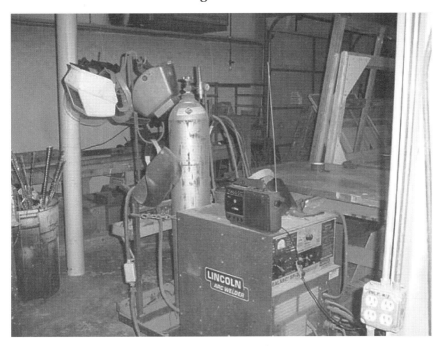

Figure 7.8.

Participant Observations, Archival Documents, and Interviews. I supplemented the unobtrusive observations with participant observations, archival documents, and interviews. On July 13, 2004, I met with the police chief and the crime prevention coordinator to discuss security issues and protocols for the clean room at NEESC. We reviewed a videotape taken on July 8 by the crime prevention coordinator that clearly showed that the clean room's emergency exit doors were propped open. These doors had been previously pried open from the outside, as evidenced by missing rubber between the doors near the lock mechanism. To further illustrate the lack of existing safety protocols at "The University" we discussed an incident that took place on July 9, 2004, in which a laser beam had accidentally hit a person in the eye. According to Staff Member No. 4, no one was seriously injured in the incident. On August 10, 2004, "The University's" environmental safety department shut down all lasers located in the clean room because the clean room did not have proper shielding over glass walls to adequately contain laser beams. It was reported by Staff Member No. 4 that laser beams were penetrating several sheets of glass and were visible on a research building located across from NEECS.

On July 22, 2004, NEECS and SEECS were evacuated due to an accident caused by an employee who, according to Staff Member No. 5, was attempting to neutralize a chemical and introduced too much of a chemical agent into the mixture, resulting in a chemical fog that filled the building. According to Staff Member No. 7, the Halon system (which uses fine dust instead of water to extinguish fires) was not deployed in the building. One person was taken to the hospital and later released. There were no documents available to inform the police department what chemical caused the fog, making it extremely difficult for the police to protect the public in this situation.

In November 2004, three engineering students were taken to a local hospital after they were exposed to a chemical that was incorrectly labeled and stored in the wrong location. According to Staff Member No. 4, it was presumed that the students were exposed to an acid that could dissolve calcium, including the calcium contained in bone. Upon examination at the hospital the three students were released since the chemical did not come in contact with their skin.

In December 2005, after a safety and procedural audit by a review committee was conducted, I interviewed Staff Member No. 9 who had responsibilities within certain research facilities at "The University." According to Staff Member No. 9, the audit revealed a potential safety concern from improper storage of chlorine gas. If the containers were damaged and leaked, chlorine gas could be released into the ventilation system, which could lead to massive chemical exposure at one research facility.

Results of the Case Study Investigation. Based on the findings of the security surveys, "The University" initiated several improvements in the way in which its research facilities are constructed and secured. The first of these improvements was initiated in 2004 with the hiring of a new environmental safety director. Staffing for the environmental safety department was increased from three employees to seven employees in 2008. The department added specializations in fire safety, industrial hygiene, occupational safety, drivers training, biological safety, laser/X-ray safety, and waste disposal. The environmental health and safety department was relocated from the waste storage depot to a new building.

The new environmental safety director reviewed and modified existing safety protocols and practices. Two older science buildings at "The University" have had emergency response guide (ERG) chemicals broken down into different categories to aid first responders in the event of an emergency. In 2007, the environmental safety director directed the shipping and receiving department to cease delivery of compressed gas cylinders to various facilities at the campus because the delivery truck was not secure enough to deliver those types of chemicals. Now the compressed gas cylinders are directly delivered to the campus facilities by the vendors ("The University" Environmental Safety Director, personal communication, 2008). Prior to 2004, there had been little thought given to tracking chemical HAZMAT at "The University." In 2008, to comply with DHS requirements, the environmental safety staff completed a substantial inventory of existing stockpiles of chemicals located in the teaching and research laboratories ("The University" Environmental Safety Director, personal communication, 2008). This information, once uploaded into "The University's" computer system, allowed authorized personnel to track laboratory chemicals, conduct audits, and respond to any crises that may occur.

Large-scale improvements have been made to campus facilities to address the heightened emphasis on HAZMAT security. In 2007, "The University" opened a new facility dedicated solely for research purposes that would house laboratories that were previously located in mixed-use buildings. By opening this new facility, research activities could be sequestered from other student areas, and research labs could be moved from old, noncompliant areas into spaces that were safer, more secure, and compliant with current regulations (Valcik, 2006). Makeshift clean rooms had been removed from an older building and relocated to this new research facility which was specifically constructed to house clean rooms ("The University" Environmental Safety Director, personal communication, 2008). The new facility contains chemical storage bunkers, storage for toxic gases for the clean room (which has a triple redundant safety), and a monitoring system ("The University" Environmental Safety

Director, personal communication, 2008). "The University" has applied this new safety consciousness to a new research facility that is to be constructed and another facility that is to be leased for research activities.

New security measures regarding chemical HAZMAT and general safety have been extended to existing facilities as well. Upon inspecting the VS building, new fireproof storage cabinets were provided to store chemicals such as acids and solvents which are used in art projects ("The University" Environmental Safety Director, personal communication, 2008). The environmental safety department also recommended that VS improve and expand its safety protocols and practices ("The University" Environmental Safety Director, personal communication, 2008). After 2004, room occupancies and fire codes have been taken more seriously with the addition of a fire safety specialist to the environmental safety department. Some facilities have had security cameras installed. While the security cameras are not IP addressable, they are an improvement over not having any security cameras at all.

As with any bureaucracy, some issues take time to resolve and "The University" is no different in this manner. This institution has not established a robust means whereby chemical HAZMAT could be electronically traced from the moment of receipt by the shipping department to its ultimate destination on campus. There was no mechanism to track compressed gas cylinders to the various locations on campus, and an effective bar coding system had not been implemented. Presently there is no campuswide security camera plan at "The University," not even for open areas such as parking lots or most building interiors. Even if there were camera coverage, there is no mechanism that would enable security forces to view the camera feed in their vehicles or on foot. According to Staff Member No. 8, some cameras had been installed in the NEECS building, but these cameras were installed only after two plasma televisions had been stolen from the engineering complex. Staff Member No. 8 also stated that a recommendation was made for mounting IP addressable cameras, but efforts to purchase and install these cameras appear to have stalled.

Conclusion

Organizational changes, new guidelines, and new techniques designed to improve safety and security take time to implement. Since my research first began in 2004, "The University" has made great strides in improving safety and addressing homeland security issues by adopting new techniques, hiring qualified personnel, and putting forth the resources necessary to stay in compliance with the new federal guidelines. To address some of these issues, "The University" will require adequate resources for new construction and modifications to existing facilities and to fund new infrastructure costs (such as security cameras) which can be quite expensive. Therefore improvements in the chemical HAZMAT situation at "The University" might take years to implement.

Although risk assessments and security surveys are often conducted by business affairs offices at most universities, such efforts can be aided, and in some cases initiated, by the institutional research office. Institutional research offices have access to personnel, student, and facilities data that can be used to analyze peak room and building use by day and hour, the ages and dimensions of research facilities, determine departmental ownership, and define facility characteristics. Analyses such as these can assist universities in modernizing facilities, tracking, and securing chemical HAZMAT, and complying with federal and state regulations. Any attempts at improving HAZMAT security can, in turn, have a positive effect on other university initiatives, such as increasing the number and dollar value of research grants, improving student and faculty recruitment endeavors, and even accreditation efforts.

References

Associated Press. "UT Lab Safety Expert Says He Was Fired for Finding Problems." *KWTX.com,* May 31, 2008. Retrieved May 12, 2010, from http://www.kwtx.com/news/headlines/19426734.html.

Barat, K. L."In Laser Safety, Little Mistakes Can Have Big Consequences." In *Photonics Spectra.* Laurin Publishing, Mar. 2005. Retrieved Apr. 21, 2008, from http://jrm.phys.ksu.edu/Safety/LaserSafety.pdf.

Becker, H. S., Geer, B., Riesman, D., and Weiss, R. S. (eds.). *Institutions and the Person: Papers Presented to Everett C. Hughes.* Chicago: Aldine, 1968.

Campbell, K. D. "MIT Panel Urges Off-Campus Sites for Classified Research; Reaffirms Openness of MIT Campus." *MIT News,* June 12, 2002.

Campus Consortium for Environmental Excellence. "EPA Launches Compliance Initiative Aimed at 258 New England Universities—Fines University of New Hampshire for Hazardous Waste Violations." Jan. 7, 2000. Retrieved Apr. 20, 2009, from http://www.c2e2.org/labxl/RCRA/region1_enforcement/region1enforcement.htm.

Christensen, K. "Deadly UCLA Lab Fire Leaves Haunting Questions." Los Angeles Times, Mar. 1, 2009. Retrieved Apr. 17, 2009, from http://www.latimes.com/news/local/la-me-uclaburn1–2009mar01,0,3624028.story?page=1.

CIDRAP. "Biodefense Research Watchdog Group Disbands." Feb. 13, 2008. Retrieved April 20, 2009, from http://www.cidrap.umn.edu/cidrap/content/bt/bioprep/news/feb1308sunshine.htm.

Department of Homeland Security. Department of Homeland Security Appropriations Act 2007: Section 550, DHS-2006–0073, RIN 1601-AA41, 6 CFR Part 27—Chemical Facility Anti-Terrorism Standards. 2007. Retrieved May 12, 2010, from http://www.dhs.gov/xlibrary/assets/IP_ChemicalFacilitySecurity.pdf.

Environmental Protection Agency (EPA). "EPA Files Complaints Against Three Universities for Hazardous Waste Violations: Columbia University, Long Island University, and New Jersey City University; Fines Total More than $1.1 Million." *News by State,* Nov. 7, 2002. Retrieved Apr. 20, 2009, from http://yosemite.epa.gov/opa/admpress.nsf/8b770facf5edf6f185257359003fb69e/37477b63d1bf5c0b85257164006 5172b!OpenDocument.

Environmental Protection Agency (EPA). "Major Enforcement Actions Against Colleges and Universities in New York, New Jersey, and the Caribbean," Region 2 Enforcement. 2008. Retrieved Apr. 20, 2009, from http://www.epa.gov/region02/p2/college/enforcement.htm.

Hilfinger, D. "UR Lab Fined for Safety Violations." *University of Rochester, Campus Times,* Mar. 5, 2009. Retrieved Apr. 17, 2009, from http://www.campustimes.org/ur-lab-fined-for-safety-violations-1.1597166.

Mount Holyoke College. "Shattuck Hall Radiation Cleanup in Progress." *The College Street Journal.* Aug. 16, 1996. Retrieved Apr. 20, 2009, from http://www.mtholyoke.edu/offices/comm/csj/960816/rad.html.

Oklahoma Higher Education. "Universities, Colleges Not Receiving Top Marks for Environmental Compliance—EPA Holding Educational Institutions to Same Standards as Industry." 2000. System Safety Health Resource Center. Retrieved Apr. 20, 2009, from http://www.okhighered.org/training-center/newsletters/osrhe/university-college-epa-compliance.html.

Oklahoma State University. "Oklahoma State University Policy and Procedures." Stillwater: Oklahoma State University, 1983.

Powers, E. "Under the Microscope." *Inside Higher Ed,* Oct. 4, 2007. Retrieved Apr. 20, 2009, from http://www.insidehighered.com/news/2007/10/04/biolabs.

Purpura, P. P. *Modern Security and Loss Prevention Management.* Burlington, Mass.: Butterworth, 1989.

Robins, M. "High Radiation Found in MIT Nuclear Worker." *Boston Globe,* Oct. 23, 2007. Retrieved Apr. 20, 2009, from http://www.boston.com/news/education/higher/articles/2007/10/23/high_radiation_found_in_mit_nuclear_worker/.

Ryder, R. W., and Gandsman, E. J. "Laboratory-Acquired Sabiá Virus Infection." *The New England Journal of Medicine,* 1995, *333*(25), 294–296. Retrieved on Apr. 20, 2009, from http://content.nejm.org/cgi/content/short/333/25/1716?query=prevarrow.

Schnirring, L. "Biosafety Lapses Reported at Three More Texas Labs." 2007. Retrieved Apr. 17, 2009, from http://www.cidrap.umn.edu/cidrap/content/bt/bioprep/news/sep1907biolab.html.

Simpson, D. "Accident at Mercer Lab Causes Explosion, Hospital Trip." *Atlanta Journal-Constitution,* Feb. 17, 2009. Retrieved Apr. 17, 2009, from http://www.ajc.com/services/content/metro/dekalb/stories/2009/02/17/mercer_lab_explosion.html?cxtype=rss&cxsvc=7&cxcat=13.

Southern California Edison. "Environmental Impact Analysis and Mitigation Measures, Tehachapi Renewable Transmission Project, Section 4.8.3.1 Regulatory Definitions." 2008. Retrieved May 12, 2010, from http://www.sce.com/nrc/trtp/PEA/4.08_HazMat.htm.

State of Texas. Texas Administrative Code, Title 1—Administration, Part 10—Department of Information Resources, Chapter 202 Information Security Standards, Subsection C—Security Standards for Institutions of Higher Education, Rule sec. 202.72, Managing Security Risks." 2008. Retrieved May 12, 2010, from http://info.sos.state.tx.us/pls/pub/readtac$ext.TacPage?sl=R&app=9&p_dir=&p_rloc=&p_tloc=&p_ploc=&pg=1&p_tac=&ti=1&pt=10&ch=202&rl=72.

Sunshine Project. "Texas A&M Bioweapons Accidents More the Norm Than an Exception." July 3, 2007. Retrieved Apr. 6, 2009, from http://www.sunshine-project.org/.

Texas A&M University–Corpus Christi. "Chemical Safety." 2004. Retrieved July 7, 2004, from http://safety.tamucc.edu/tamucc/chemical.html.

Tulane University Health Sciences Center. "Hazardous Materials and Waste. OEHS Policies." Medford, Mass.: Tufts University, 2004.

Union Carbide. "Bhopal Information Center: Chronology." 2007. Retrieved May 12, 2010, from http://www.bhopal.com/chrono.htm.

University of Maine. *Environmental Health and Safety Manual*. Orono: University of Maine, 2004.

University of New Brunswick, Office of Campus Safety, "Laboratory Safety." 2004. Retrieved May 12, 2010, from http://www.unb.ca/safety/labsafety.html.

University of Texas at Arlington. "Chemical and Biological Laboratory Safety." 2004. Retrieved May 12, 2010, from http://www.uta.edu/policy/forms/ehs/11biochm.pdf.

Valcik, N. A. *Regulating the Use of Biological Hazardous Materials in Universities: Complying with the New Federal Guidelines*. Lewiston, N.Y.: Edwin Mellen Press, 2006.

Vasich, T. "Independent Investigations Lists Causes Behind Fire at UCI's Reines Hall." *UC Newsroom*, Feb. 1, 2002. Retrieved Apr. 17, 2009, from http://www .universityofcalifornia.edu/news/article/3934.

Wikipedia. "Nuclear and Radiation Accidents." 2009. Retrieved Apr. 17, 2009, from http://en.wikipedia.org/wiki/List_of_nuclear_accidents#Civilian_nuclear_accidents.

Yale University. "Guidelines for Safe Laboratory Practices." Department of Chemistry. 2004. Retrieved May 12, 2010, from http://www.chem.yale.edu/safety/ SafetyManual04.pdf.

NICOLAS A. VALCIK is the associate director for the Office of Strategic Planning and Analysis and an assistant clinical professor for the Program of Public Affairs at The University of Texas at Dallas.

8

This chapter explores the relationship between homeland security incidents and the impact that those incidents have on enrollment at higher education institutions.

Impact of Incidents on Enrollments at Higher Education Institutions

Hans P. L'Orange

Higher education is a remarkably consistent enterprise. The same general pattern, by and large, has existed since the enactment of the G.I. Bill in 1944 and large numbers of returning veterans began enrolling in American higher education. Although the definition of a traditional student is changing, many students still enroll in the fall to begin four or more years of college. The number of students enrolling has climbed steadily according to the U.S. Department of Education: "Enrollment in degree-granting institutions increased by 16 percent between 1985 and 1995. Between 1995 and 2005, enrollment increased at a faster rate (23 percent), from 14.3 million to 17.5 million" (U.S. Department of Education, 2008).

This is not surprising, as the value of a college degree continues to be demonstrated. The average real income for males in 2008, as collected by the Census Bureau and reported by Postsecondary Education Opportunity (www.postsecondary.org), was $37,413 for high school graduates and almost double ($74,307) for men with a bachelor's degree. Barring unforeseen circumstances, this trend is likely to continue. One circumstance that has the potential to affect enrollment is incidents of catastrophic proportion.

NEW DIRECTIONS FOR INSTITUTIONAL RESEARCH, no. 146, Summer 2010 © Wiley Periodicals, Inc.
Published online in Wiley InterScience (www.interscience.wiley.com) • DOI: 10.1002/ir.346

Catastrophes at Higher Education Institutions

Catastrophes at higher education institutions occur with unfortunate frequency. There have been forty-two shootings with fatalities in U.S. schools and colleges between August 1, 1966, when Charles Whitman opened fire from Austin Tower at the University of Texas, and April 16, 2007, when Seung-Hui Cho killed 32 people at Virginia Tech. Over 150 people have been killed and numerous others have been wounded in these incidents. Many are familiar to the American public (among them, those at Columbine, Colorado, and Red Lake Indian Reservation, Minnesota), but many others are less well known (Virginia Tech Review Panel, 2007).

Natural disasters like the flooding of the Iowa River in June 2008 and Hurricane Katrina in August 2005 also have affected many campuses and students. Katrina was particularly notable, with 80 percent of the city of New Orleans under water and many students displaced. Tulane University had a damage estimate of $200 million following Hurricane Katrina, and the University of New Orleans reported damage amounting to $103 million. Several campuses lost 50 percent or more of their enrollment. Negative publicity, the loss of faculty and staff, and a decrease in donor support also were widely felt. Sports teams played every game on the road, and valuable research material was lost (Mytelka, 2006).

Impact on Students

Hurricane Katrina forced over fifty thousand students to evacuate their campuses, and many of these enrolled at other institutions. A paper prepared for the 2006 annual meeting of the Southern Sociological Society (Ladd, Marszalek, and Gill, 2006) provides a summary to a survey sent to the student bodies of Loyola University, Xavier University, and the University of New Orleans:

- 81 percent had their on- or off-campus housing damaged, and 40.8 percent said they were unable to continue living in that place of residence
- 84.6 percent reported they had incurred some financial loss
- 39.4 percent indicated they had lost their job
- almost 75 percent of the respondents believed that it was "somewhat," "very," or "definitely likely" that their academic performance had been negatively affected
- 36.3 percent of the responding students noted they had withdrawn from classes for which they had enrolled after the hurricane hit
- 55.2 percent reported they had been unable to contact their advisors

The impact on these students clearly was significant. The long-term impact on the institutions in the affected area is somewhat harder

Table 8.1. Enrollment Data for Loyola University, Xavier University, and the University of New Orleans, Before and After Hurricane Katrina

Student Level	2004	2005	2006	2007
Less than two years (below associate)	5,167	5,096	4,199	4,260
At least two years but less than four years	60,530	39,849	55,627	61,483
Four or more years	194,447	160,262	173,305	169,388
Louisiana total	260,144	205,207	233,331	235,131

Source: U.S. Department of Education (2008).

to quantify. Aggregate state-level data from the National Center for Education Statistics (NCES) provides some insight into the general trends for the fall enrollment in the years immediately before and after the August 2005 storm.

Although there are certainly differences in the general trends from campus to campus depending on specific circumstances, it is apparent that an enrollment pattern is emerging for Louisiana as a whole. Enrollment dropped immediately and significantly after the hurricane, as would be expected with the huge loss of facilities and staff. Enrollment was well below the prehurricane level of 2004 in the year following the hurricane, but then it climbed above those first-year numbers in the next year (2007) for which national data are available. Enrollment has not reached the levels seen in 2004 but started to climb back up from the initial days immediately following the hurricanes of 2005 (see Table 8.1).

Institutions are certainly not back to their pre-Katrina enrollment levels, but indicators are encouraging. Reports from institutions indicate students are starting to return to New Orleans. Although national enrollment data are not yet available for 2008–09, Tulane, Loyola, and Xavier all had significant increases in both applications and enrollment in their 2008 freshman classes. Xavier expected a 20 percent increase in its freshman population over 2007, and Loyola planned for a 44 percent increase. Tulane's applications were at an all-time high for fall 2008, with 34,100 students expressing interest in the university compared with 17,572 for the year prior to the hurricane. Tulane's vice president for enrollment reports that "kids are coming down intent on getting the city back on its feet" (Jervis, 2008). Universities have been aggressive in their recruiting. Loyola's vice president for enrollment management notes:

> We have told this university's story with the help of our creative and committed community. Visitors receive an authentic, three-dimensional experience when they come see us. . . . We believe very strongly in Loyola and communicate this vision to prospective students. We are thrilled the

NEW DIRECTIONS FOR INSTITUTIONAL RESEARCH • DOI: 10.1002/ir

message has taken root and that so many students are discovering that a Loyola education fits their needs. . . . The staff in admissions and financial aid worked very hard to achieve these results. Our enrollment team builds strong relationships with families and students and this is followed up with great tours and faculty who take the time to sit down with families and make phone calls to prospective students [Loyola University, 2009].

In 2007, the Louisiana commissioner of higher education, Joseph Savoie, noted that the state's public institutions were "still down about 16,000 students overall compared to pre-storm enrollments. That's one of the reasons why we've taken several measures this year to attract more students of all ages to our campuses." Those measures included new financial aid programs for low- to moderate-income students, an adult learning initiative, and the expansion of dual-enrollment programs for high school students (Louisiana Board of Regents, 2007).

The impact of violence on Virginia Tech and the flooding at the University of Iowa were certainly traumatic but were not reflected in their enrollment numbers. Summer classes in Iowa were disrupted, and the facilities experienced severe damage, but classes proceeded on a comparatively normal basis in the fall. Iowa's entering fall 2008 enrollment was the third highest, and total enrollment was a record, with 30,561 students on campus despite the flood earlier in the summer and some facilities still under renovation (University of Iowa, 2008b).

The massacre at Virginia Tech in April 2007 appeared to have little effect on enrollment as the university exceeded its enrollment goals for the fall 2007 freshmen class. In the month following the shooting, only two new students withdrew their deposits because of the incident, and one other admitted applicant chose not to attend. As one student said, "I don't think the school's unsafe. What happened can happen anywhere" (Hoover, 2007). Enrollment for fall 2007 was 27,572 students compared with 26,371 for the previous fall. Fall 2008 on-campus enrollment was higher yet, at 28,259 (Virginia Tech University, 2009).

Northern Illinois University is another institution that experienced the tragedy of an armed gunman opening fire on students. Enrollment did decrease 3.4 percent at the University of Northern Illinois from fall 2007 to fall 2008. However, it is difficult to attribute the drop of 486 enrolled students to the negative impact of the February 14, 2008, shooting. Campus officials note that undergraduate applicants for the semester actually were up over 1,000 from the prior year, and the number of students who confirmed their intent to enroll was similarly higher than the 2007 numbers. Concerns over the economy and decisions to enroll in lower-cost regional community colleges appear to have a greater impact on students than do fears over campus safety (Northern Illinois University, 2008).

Institutional and State Responses to Catastrophes

The University of Iowa revised its summer calendar in response to the devastation caused by the flooding of the Iowa River. Other campus responses included revising graduate academic deadlines, rescheduling new student orientation programs, and relocating classes to different buildings (University of Iowa, 2008a). In addition, a flood relief fund was established by the Iowa College Student Aid Commission to assist college and university students across the state who were affected by the flooding and other natural disasters, including numerous tornados, that occurred that summer. A scholarship and tuition grant reserve fund made $500,000 available. Nearly 700 people applied for them, and 414 students from thirty-nine Iowa colleges and universities were determined to have met previously established qualifications (Greiner, 2008).

The response to the tragic shootings at Virginia Tech took a different direction as befitting the nature of the catastrophe. "Hundreds of individuals and dozens of agencies . . . mobilized to provide assistance." Immediate action by the university following the shootings focused on providing "support to the families of Virginia Tech students and particularly to the family members of the slain and injured" (Virginia Tech Review Panel, 2007, pp. 135–136). At least as important, campuses across the country evaluated their emergency procedures, notification systems, and student policies. Many have implemented new or enhanced procedures to improve communication and mobilize emergency crews (Rasmussen and Johnson, 2008). The shootings also brought increased attention to the Family Educational Rights and Privacy Act of 1974 (FERPA). Particular attention was focused on "the often difficult task of balancing individual privacy rights with the need to communicate with appropriate authorities when a student exhibits disturbing or threatening behavior" (Rasmussen and Johnson, 2008, p. 13).

Louisiana had a substantially larger disaster to deal with—one that extended far beyond the campuses of the state's colleges and universities. Millions of dollars flowed from the state and the federal government to address the damage and begin the process of rebuilding. Outpouring of support from institutions around the country resulted in schools' and colleges' opening their doors to displaced students, often waiving tuition and other fees. Many states also quickly established or modified policies to help these students. Kentucky's postsecondary institutions responded to students displaced by Hurricane Katrina by offering tuition waivers to those who had already paid tuition at their home institution; others were evaluated on a case-by-case basis. Offers of office and lab space for displaced faculty, extensive fundraising drives, and the development of online courses are a few other examples of institutional efforts (Kentucky Council on Postsecondary Education, 2005).

Many Texas institutions provided support to many students from neighboring Louisiana. The University of Houston enrolled approximately 1,400 students after the university deadline at in-state tuition rates, Brookhaven College provided in-district tuition to 286 students, Rice University enrolled 106 Houston-area students as emergency visiting students, and Southern Methodist University enrolled 300 students from Tulane University (Campus Compact, 2009).

The University of Oklahoma extended admission deadlines and provided advisement and enrollment assistance to displaced students. OU provided nonresident tuition waivers for displaced students who were nonresidents and extensive financial aid counseling; moreover, expedited processing was available, and housing was offered to displaced students (Oklahoma State Regents, 2005).

Brown University used $1.1 million of philanthropist Sidney E. Frank's $5 million hurricane relief gift to establish "recovery semester" scholarships for students at Dillard University and Xavier University of Louisiana and Tougaloo College in Mississippi. The scholarships were designed to help students resume or continue their studies and help provide the schools with sufficient numbers of students to begin the return to normal operations (Brown University, 2005).

A particularly innovative response to Hurricane Katrina used online learning to provide students around the country with access to free online courses. A grant of $1.1 million from the Alfred P. Sloan Foundation created the Sloan Semester, a fully functional virtual university, in only twenty-one days. The following statistics outline the extent of the Sloan Semester's impact:

- 153 institutions offered 1,345 fully online courses.
- 800 courses offered by 135 institutions from 36 states wound up enrolling Sloan Semester students.
- 4,114 seats were requested by students.
- 1,736 students applied to the Sloan Semester, and 1,587 were admitted.
- More than 9,000 enrollments were processed in Sloan Semester courses.
- Some of the courses enrolled only Sloan Semester students, and others enrolled a mix of Sloan Semester students with the institution's native students.
- Participating institutions contributed (forgave) more than $3.1 million in tuition and fee dollars.

The Sloan Semester was designed as a bridge to allow students to continue their education and then return to their home institution (Sloan-C, 2009). The focus was on the students, and as Bruce Chaloux, director of the electronic campus for the Southern Regional Education Board, said in numerous post-Katrina presentations, "We established rules to benefit them, we 'pushed' institutions to agree to keep the focus on them, and we sought to lessen the academic 'red tape' on them."

Conclusion

Identifying parallels between catastrophic events is problematic; the very nature of a catastrophe is that each event has unique characteristics. Moreover, analyzing the impact on students and institutional behavior following campus incidents is difficult. This is not meant to minimize the impact catastrophes have on students, whether it is a shooting that shocks a campus or a national disaster that displaces thousands and shuts entire campuses across a state. Students suffered severe and long-term emotional grief and, in some cases, physical pain in the shootings at Virginia Tech University and Northern Illinois University. For some, the consequences are likely always to be with them. Thousands of students were displaced in Louisiana and Mississippi as a result of Hurricanes Katrina and Rita. Possessions were lost forever, and studies were clearly disrupted. Many students did not return to their colleges and universities, but others, including many new students, did enroll in successive terms. The admissions numbers of new students would seem to imply the impact is greatest on existing students; new students are not deterred from pursuing their future educational dreams as a result of past events.

Drawing conclusions is risky, and more research is clearly warranted to fully understand student enrollment behavior around catastrophes, but incidents on specific campuses appear to have limited impact on student behavior. Some students may be lost to higher education, but overall enrollment climbs regardless of a shooting or flood that affects but does not close a campus like the University of Iowa. In cases where the entire community is affected and a campus is unable to open, there is an understandable, and likely unavoidable, decrease in enrollment in the period immediately following the catastrophe. However, the impact seems to be minimized through the efforts of campus, state, and federal administrators and policy makers.

Another interesting question worthy of additional research is what the impact on enrollment would have been if these efforts had not been instituted. If students had not been able to enroll in alternate institutions at in-state tuition rates, if grants for living expenses had not been available, or if online learning had not been available, how many more students would have been lost to higher education? It is likely the enrollment downturn would have been even more severe, and many more students would not have enrolled in 2006.

Unforeseen and catastrophic events do have an effect, but the overall impact on enrollment appears to be either minimized or short-lived. Enrollment trend numbers start from a new, lower base but climb back up, showing us that students and institutions are remarkably resilient.

NEW DIRECTIONS FOR INSTITUTIONAL RESEARCH • DOI: 10.1002/ir

References

Brown University. "$1.1M of Sidney Frank Gift Will Fund 'Recovery Semester' Scholarships." Dec. 21, 2005. Retrieved June 23, 2009, from http://www.brown.edu/Administration/News_Bureau/2005–06/05–056.html.

Campus Compact. "Higher Education Responds to Katrina." 2005. Retrieved June 23, 2009, from http://www.compact.org/wp-content/uploads/resources/downloads/Katrina.pdf.

Greiner, K. "Response to Statewide Disasters of 2008." Iowa College Student Aid Commission, Nov. 2008.

Hoover, E. "Virginia Tech Exceeds Enrollment Goal for Next Fall's Freshman Class." *Chronicle of Higher Education*, May 11, 2007. Retrieved June 23, 2009, from http://chronicle.com/daily/2007/05/2007051706n.htm.

Jervis, R. "Freshmen Flock to New Orleans." *USA Today*, Aug. 30, 2008.

Kentucky Council on Postsecondary Education. "News and Updates: Kentucky Postsecondary Education System Responds to Students Displaced by Hurricane Katrina." 2005. Retrieved June 23, 2009, from http://cpe.ky.gov/katrina.htm.

Ladd, A. E., Marszalek, J., and Gill, D. "The Other Diaspora: New Orleans Student Evacuation Impacts and Responses Surrounding Hurricane Katrina." Paper presented at the Annual Meeting of the Southern Sociological Society, New Orleans, Mar. 22–26, 2006.

Louisiana Board of Regents. "Statewide Postsecondary Enrollment Recovery Continues." Press release, Sept. 26, 2007.

Loyola University. "Initial Freshmen Enrollment Figures Promise Strong Fall for Loyola." Press release, May 26, 2009.

Mytelka, A. "Colleges Begin to Reopen in New Orleans as Higher Education Reveals a Face Much Changed by Katrina." *Chronicle of Higher Education*, Jan. 11, 2006. Retrieved June 23, 2009, from chronicle.com/daily/2006/01/2006011101n.htm.

Northern Illinois University. "NIU Tenth-Day Enrollment Figures Released." Press release, Sept. 11, 2008.

Oklahoma State Regents for Higher Education. "Oklahoma Higher Education Responds to Students Affected by Hurricane Katrina." 2005. Retrieved June 23, 2009, from http://www.okhighered.org/news-center/katrina-response.shtml.

Rasmussen, C., and Johnson, G. "The Ripple Effect of Virginia Tech: Assessing the Nationwide Impact on Campus Safety and Security Policy and Practice." Minneapolis: Midwestern Higher Education Compact, 2008.

Sloan-C. "The Sloan Semester." 2009. Retrieved June 23, 2009, from http://www.aln.org/sloansemester/index.asp.

University of Iowa. "Flood Information Blog," June 25, 2008a. Retrieved June 23, 2009, from http://uiflood.blogspot.com/.

University of Iowa. "Total Enrollment Up at UI for 2008 Fall Semester." News release, Sept. 10, 2008b.

U.S. Department of Education, National Center for Education Statistics. Digest of Education Statistics, 2007. Washington, D.C.: U.S. Department of Education, 2008.

Virginia Tech Review Panel. "Report." 2007. Retrieved June 23, 2009, from http://www.vtreviewpanel.org/.

Virginia Tech University, Office of Institutional Research and Effectiveness. "Current Enrollment Summaries." Feb, 25, 2009. Retrieved June 23, 2009, from http://www.ir.vt.edu/VT_Stats/enrollments_contents.htm#EN1.

HANS P. L'ORANGE *is the vice president for research and information resources and director of the State Higher Education Executive Officers/NCES Network.*

NEW DIRECTIONS FOR INSTITUTIONAL RESEARCH • DOI: 10.1002/ir

9 *This chapter summarizes the previous chapters and discusses the impact of homeland security mandates on higher education institutions' operations.*

Conclusion

Dawn Kenney

"Homeland security refers to a security effort by a government to protect a nation against perceived external or internal threats" (Wikipedia). After the attacks of 9/11 in the United States, following the merger of several government agencies, the Department of Homeland Security was formed (Homeland Security Act of 2002). The National Strategy for Homeland Security released in October 2007 defines four goals:

Prevent and disrupt terrorist attacks;
Protect the American people, our critical infrastructure, and key resources;
Respond to and recover from incidents that do occur; and
Continue to strengthen the foundation to ensure our long-term success.

After the attacks of 9/11, two major pieces of legislation were passed intending to shore up gaps in America's security (see Chapter Five). These legislation were the Public Health Security and Bioterrorism Preparedness and Response Act (2002) and the USA PATRIOT Act. The Patriot Act has some provisions that impact the Family Educational Rights and Privacy Act (FERPA), the Electronic Communications Privacy Act, the Foreign Intelligence Surveillance Act (FISA), the Student and Visitor Exchange System (SEVIS), and others that do not relate directly to higher education (Mitrano, 2002). Both pieces of legislation have impacts on institutions of higher education.

In this volume, the issues discussed fall into three broad categories:

- Protection of data from within the institution, that is, statistical confidentiality
- Protection of data from outside the institution: security breaches from server breaches, software applications, and information left on laptops, for example
- Campus security, which refers to criminal background checks, SEVIS, GIS, and compliance issues

How do institutions implement all of this? Do the benefits of implementation exceed the costs? Are these unfunded federal mandates? An unfunded mandate must meet two criteria. A mandate is "any provision in legislation, statute, or regulation that would impose an enforceable duty on state, local, or tribal governments . . . or that would reduce or eliminate the amount of funding authorized to cover the costs of existing mandates. Duties that arise as a condition of federal assistance or from participating in a voluntary federal program are not mandates" (Riedl, 2003). To be unfunded, a mandate must meet the following criteria: "Direct federal funding is less than the amount state, local, and tribal governments would be required to spend to comply with the mandate. Such costs are limited to spending that result directly from the enforceable duty imposed by the legislation rather than from the legislation's broad effects on the economy. An unfunded mandate does not violate UMRA [Unfunded Mandates Reform Act] unless the combined annual cost to state, local and tribal governments exceeds $58 million (inflation-adjusted from $50 million in 1996), which is approximately $1.2 million per state" (Riedl, 2003).

"The Unfunded Mandates Reform Act of 1995 (UMRA) was enacted to address concerns about federal, state, local, and tribal governments or the private sector to expend resources to achieve legislative goals" (U.S. General Accounting Office, 2004). The purpose of the act was to curb the practice of imposing unfunded federal mandates on private or governmental entities without adequate funding and to ensure that the federal government pays the costs incurred by those entities in complying with certain requirements. A requirement is that congressional committees estimate the costs that passing the bill would place on private and governmental entities (Robinson, 2005). If the expenses are estimated to be greater than $58 million a year, then there needs to be a congressional majority agreeing that the benefit outweighs the cost. In other words, an unfunded federal mandate is a federal law that imposes some kind of expenditure in order to be in compliance, but there is a threshold that must be met. In this time of belt tightening, any mandate, technically funded or not, that incurs a cost to a college or university is in effect an unfunded mandate in the institution's eyes.

When a college or university is forced to comply with a seemingly unfunded federal mandate, resources must be allocated from other needed areas. Homeland Security and the Patriot Act are just two that appear to be unfunded mandates. According to the Congressional Budget Office (CBO), there have been only two significant unfunded mandates imposed on state and local governments since 1996: the minimum wage increase and the reimbursement reduction for food stamps administrative changes, which are to cost each state approximately $9 million per year. The Congressional Budget Office does not consider either the Homeland Security Act or the Patriot Act to be unfunded mandates, which are considered to have marginal to no cost to state budgets.

Protection of data from within the institution, in the form of statistical confidentiality, is reviewed in Chapter Two. Protection of individual identifying information is extremely important while performing research, but during times of crisis, information sharing needs to be tempered with good policies that govern this. Researchers need to be aware of the laws regulating the protection of information to protect the individual as well as the institution and themselves.

As discussed in Chapter Three, informational security threats from outside the institution have increased over time, and institutions have had to react to these threats. Server breaches, laptop thefts, and software applications with hidden vulnerabilities have all contributed to security issues. This forces many institutions to constantly upgrade servers, software, and computers and hire more staff to keep up with the ever changing information technology landscape. Many institutions and institutional research offices maintain huge amounts of data on the main network and server system. A security breach could leave a thief with enough information to steal the identity of thousands of individuals. The annual cost to an institution to keep up with all the necessary information technology safeguards is significant. While an argument could be made that the college would have needed to do this anyway, it could also be argued that federal mandates since 9/11 have necessitated increased protection of information and therefore increased the cost.

Campus security continues to be a topic of great concern to institutions. It will never be possible to create a 100 percent safe campus, and no campus is invincible, but we can strive for as safe a campus as possible. As discussed in Chapter Four, the use of criminal background checks for more than applicants in sensitive positions has increased as campus safety and security have increased. In October 2004, the rate for a combined Department of Justice and Federal Bureau of Investigation report was eighty-two dollars per person. The cost to the college can be significant because of the number of people who work in sensitive positions, coupled with possible yearly background checks. Who can put a dollar amount on the benefit? How does the benefit of preventing future incidents get calculated?

SEVIS was declared a success with the Bush administration, yet some colleges and universities may not agree. In 2004, the American Association of Collegiate Registrars and Admission Officers (AACRAO) conducted a survey to gauge the satisfaction level of member institutions that participate in SEVIS (AACRAO, 2004). It concluded that SEVIS has significantly increased or somewhat increased the workload for over 80 percent of respondents; many institutions that participate reported receiving no training; over half experience functionality and data integrity issues; and international student recruitment and enrollment have suffered. Chapter Five reports consultations with staff at four colleges and universities. The author discovered that compliance for some is time-consuming and costly, while for others it is straightforward. She also found that compliance is frustrating for college employees as "near continuous change plagues the system and challenges individuals who must make the system work." One college also reported that the cost of SEVIS limits its ability to recruit international students more aggressively because less money is available for this purpose. This appears to be consistent with results from the SEVIS survey as well. SEVIS sets out many rules and regulations, and the institution must continue to budget for licensing and maintenance costs. Institutions can also lose federal funding and education grants and scholarships for noncompliance. In 2003, the assistant vice chancellor for budget resource management at the University of California at Davis said, "To meet federal demands on tracking international student and scholar information, the campus will spend more than $310,000 on one-time costs and $184,267 in on-going costs for new software in the year ahead" (Parker, 2003).

Geographic information systems (GIS), the topic of Chapter Six, are extremely useful in campus security and emergency management and have proven to be an asset to adopters of the technology. It has been recognized as a need by the Department of Homeland Security to have ready in case of any type of incident. Institutions can create GIS databases to assist with campus and emergency management. However, GIS have high learning curves and are expensive when one considers the tightening of higher education institutional budgets over the past few years. An institution must also take into account usability, staff training, support, and other costs such as any services and data when determining the benefit to the institution. One resource that can be tapped is faculty proficient in the use of GIS.

The Chemical Facility Anti-Terrorism Standards of the Department of Homeland Security Appropriations Act of 2007 is addressed by Nicolas Valcik in Chapter Seven, which focuses on chemical HAZMAT. These issues can have a great impact on campus security. Because most institutional research offices are responsible for state and federal reporting, they too may be affected by these regulations if they are to provide chemical HAZMAT reporting. Noncompliance can result in funding cuts, fines, criminal charges, and other sanctions. A case study as part of research into HAZMAT security issues is included in this chapter. The case study resulted in improvements to "the university" research facilities. Again, the impact and cost of complying with the new standards are potentially enormous. Where does "The University" find these funds? As previously stated, the Homeland Security Act is not considered an unfunded mandate and the impact to states and higher education institutions marginal. But, as we see in this chapter, there is the potential for great expenses for "the university" to comply with the new standards. However, the benefit to the university can be just as great in the form of new research grants and dollars flowing into the university. Information from the University of New Mexico confirmed that there is indeed no federal funding for SEVIS.

As we have seen, the effect of an officially unfunded mandate or a seemingly unfunded mandate can have a great impact on institutions of higher education. The cost of compliance can be significant. "The Patriot Act covers a wide range of activities on university campuses. Some of the activities it covers include putting restrictions on certain biological agents and toxins that can be in research labs around campus and limiting the research activities of international students and other 'restricted persons'" (Parker, 2003). In 2003, the assistant vice chancellor for research administration at the University of California at Davis said that the Patriot Act alone and various other homeland security rules would cost the campus "a couple million dollars" to implement. In fact, the university might have to go above and beyond to comply with apparent unfunded mandates, but the cost of noncompliance can be too severe. This may be true for most institutions, especially those that do research.

Do all the homeland security mandates make higher education institutions safer in some way, funded or otherwise? And is the return on investment for the amount spent by institutions to be in compliance a value? It can be argued that the answer is that some mandates are beneficial, and others appear to be detrimental. SEVIS is the responsibility of each institution to fund and helps make campuses safer. Yet according to the 2007 Student Pulse Survey from the International Graduate Insight Group, the United States is losing ground to Britain as the most popular destination for overseas students. Of course, background checks can help avert future incidents, which should be counted positive for safety.

References

American Association of Collegiate Registrars and Admission Officers (AACRAO). "SEVIS Survey." American Association of Collegiate Registrars and Admission Officers, 2004.

Mitrano, T. "Taking the Mystique Out of the USA-Patriot Act: Information, Process, and Protocol." Ithaca, N.Y.: Cornell University IT Policy Office, 2002.

Parker, C. B. "Unfunded Mandates Keep Campus and UC Walking Fine Line." *Dateline UC Davis*, April 11, 2003.

Riedl, B. "What Unfunded Mandates? CBO Study Reveals Washington Not at Fault for State Budget Crises." *The Heritage Foundation*, Webmemo #283, May 28, 2003. Retrieved May 18, 2010, from http://www.heritage.org/Research/Reports/2003/06/What-Unfunded-Mandates-CBO-Study-Reveals-Washington-Not-at-Fault-for-State-Budget-Crises.

NEW DIRECTIONS FOR INSTITUTIONAL RESEARCH • DOI: 10.1002/ir

Robinson, G. "Unfunded Mandates and 'Uncontrollables.'" *Gotham Gazette: New York City News and Policy*, May 30, 2005.

U.S. General Accounting Office. "Unfunded Mandates: Analysis of Reform Act Coverage. Report to the Chairman, Subcommittee on Oversight of Government Management, the Federal Workforce, and the District of Columbia, Committee on Governmental Affairs, U.S. Senate." Washington, D.C.: U.S. General Accounting Office, 2004.

DAWN KENNEY *is the director of planning and institutional research for Central New Mexico Community College.*

INDEX

reorganize their existing programs, structures, and patterns. This too may demand more of institutional research. A decade ago, M. W. Peterson proposed in volume 104 of *New Directions for Institutional Research* that the future challenge for institutional research would be not only to help institutions improve but to help facilitate their redesign and transformation. It appears that time has arrived. At most institutions, however, for institutional research to play such a substantive role, the field will need to redesign and transform itself. In this volume, the editor and authors take a proactive, strategic stance by imagining the future of institutional research and how to achieve it.
ISBN: 978-04705-69269

IR 142   **Conducting Research on Asian Americans in Higher Education**
Samuel D. Museus
This volume of *New Directions for Institutional Research* moves beyond pervasive oversimplified and preconceived notions about Asian Americans in higher education and offers new directions in studying this population. The authors highlight the complexities inherent in the realities of Asian Americans in higher education. In addition to deconstructing common misconceptions that lead to the invisibility of Asian Americans in higher education research, they discuss methodological issues related to disaggregating data, assessing programmatic interventions, conducting campus climate research, engaging Asian American undergraduates in the research process, and using critical perspectives related to Asian Americans. They also discuss key challenges and future directions in research on this population.
ISBN: 978-04705-29614

IR 141   **Using NSSE in Institutional Research**
Robert M. Gonyea, George D. Kuh
Student engagement is now part of the higher education lexicon in North America. This *New Directions for Institutional Research* volume explains the value and relevance of the construct, with an emphasis on how results from the National Survey of Student Engagement have been used for various purposes. Because process indicators are often used as proxy measures for institutional quality, the chapter authors discuss how student engagement data can help colleges and universities satisfy the demand for more evidence, accountability, and transparency of student and institutional performance. The widespread uses of student engagement results have helped to increase the visibility and importance of campus assessment efforts and of institutional researchers, who provide campus leaders with objective, trustworthy data about student and institutional performance.
ISBN: 978-04704-99283

IR 140   **Using Financial and Personnel Data in a Changing World for Institutional Research**
Nicolas A. Valcik
This volume of *New Directions for Institutional Research* explores the ways in which financial and human resource data can be used in reporting and analysis. With public sources of revenue stagnating or declining and tuition costs increasing, the need for improved efficiencies in an institution's internal practices has become paramount. An institutional research department can use financial and human resource data to conduct analyses of institutional business practices to forecast costs and identify revenue generation. The chapter authors review the use of personnel, expenditure, and revenue data in the performance of institutional research from several perspectives: the role of organizational theory in data mining efforts, integration of various data sources for effective analyses, methodologies

for more efficient faculty compensation benchmarking, the impact of state legislative decisions on revenue streams, and return on investment calculations.
ISBN: 978-04704-68517

IR139   **Conducting Institutional Research in Non-Campus-Based Settings**
Robert K. Toutkoushian, Tod R. Massa
One aspect of the institutional research (IR) profession that has not been well documented is the many ways that this research is carried out beyond the confines of a traditional campus-based IR office. The purpose of this volume of *New Directions for Institutional Research* is to provide readers with insight into some of these alternatives and help expand understanding of the nature of institutional research. The chapters in this volume show how institutional research is being conducted by public university system offices, state higher education coordinating boards, institutional-affiliated research offices, and higher education consultants. Because these entities often do not have ready access to campus-specific data, they must be creative in finding ways to obtain data and information that enable them to provide a value-added function in the field. The chapter authors highlight ways in which these offices acquire and use information for institutional research.
ISBN: 978-04704-12749

IR138   **Legal Applications of Data for Institutional Research**
Andrew L. Luna
This volume of *New Directions for Institutional Research* explores the seemingly incongruent forces of statistical reasoning and the law and sheds some light on how institutional researchers can use the two in a complementary manner to prevent a legal action or to help support the rebuttal of a prima facie case (i.e., one that at first glance presents sufficient evidence for the plaintiff to win the case). Until now, there has been little linkage between the disciplines of law and statistics. While the legal profession uses statistics to support an argument, interpretations of statistical outcomes may not follow scientific reasoning. Similarly, a great piece of statistical theory or a tried-and-true methodology among institutional research professionals may be thrown out of court if it fails to meet the rules of evidence or contradicts current legal standing. The information contained within this volume will benefit institutional research practitioners and contribute to a more frequent dialogue concerning the complexities of statistical science within the legal environment.
ISBN: 978-04703-97619

IR137   **Alternative Perspectives in Institutional Planning**
Terry T. Ishitani
Institutional planning is coming to the fore in higher education as states, the federal government, and the public increasingly demand accountability. Institutional researchers, the data stewards for colleges and universities, are becoming involved in such strategic planning, supporting efforts to strengthen institutional efficiency and effectiveness in policymaking. Researchers find that locating, preparing, and presenting necessary data and information for planners is a challenging exercise. In this volume of *New Directions for Institutional Research*, administrators, consultants, researchers, and scholars provide unique, innovative approaches to that challenge. Some authors introduce program applications and statistical techniques; others share case studies. The variety of perspectives and depths of focus makes this a timely, useful guide for institutional researchers.
ISBN: 978-04703-84534

NEW DIRECTIONS FOR INSTITUTIONAL RESEARCH
ORDER FORM SUBSCRIPTION AND SINGLE ISSUES

DISCOUNTED BACK ISSUES:

Use this form to receive 20% off all back issues of *New Directions for Institutional Research*.
All single issues priced at **$23.20** (normally $29.00)

TITLE	ISSUE NO.	ISBN

Call 888-378-2537 or see mailing instructions below. When calling, mention the promotional code JBNND to receive your discount. For a complete list of issues, please visit www.josseybass.com/go/ndir

SUBSCRIPTIONS: (1 YEAR, 4 ISSUES)

☐ New Order   ☐ Renewal

U.S.	☐ Individual: $100	☐ Institutional: $280
CANADA/MEXICO	☐ Individual: $100	☐ Institutional: $320
ALL OTHERS	☐ Individual: $124	☐ Institutional: $354

Call 888-378-2537 or see mailing and pricing instructions below.
Online subscriptions are available at www.onlinelibrary.wiley.com

ORDER TOTALS:

Issue / Subscription Amount: $ _____

Shipping Amount: $ _____
(for single issues only – subscription prices include shipping)

Total Amount: $ _____

SHIPPING CHARGES:
First Item $5.00
Each Add'l Item $3.00

(No sales tax for U.S. subscriptions. Canadian residents, add GST for subscription orders. Individual rate subscriptions must be paid by personal check or credit card. Individual rate subscriptions may not be resold as library copies.)

BILLING & SHIPPING INFORMATION:

☐ **PAYMENT ENCLOSED:** *(U.S. check or money order only. All payments must be in U.S. dollars.)*

☐ **CREDIT CARD:** ☐ VISA ☐ MC ☐ AMEX

Card number _____ Exp. Date _____

Card Holder Name _____ Card Issue # _____

Signature _____ Day Phone _____

☐ **BILL ME:** *(U.S. institutional orders only. Purchase order required.)*

Purchase order # _____
Federal Tax ID 13559302 • GST 89102-8052

Name _____

Address _____

Phone _____ E-mail _____

Copy or detach page and send to: **John Wiley & Sons, PTSC, 5th Floor**
989 Market Street, San Francisco, CA 94103-1741

Order Form can also be faxed to: **888-481-2665**

PROMO JBNND